TWAYNE'S WORLD AUTHORS SERIES

A Survey of the World's Literature

Sylvia E. Bowman, Indiana University
GENERAL EDITOR

RUSSIA

Nicholas P. Vaslef, U.S. Air Force Academy
EDITOR

Ivan Goncharov

(TWAS 200)

TWAYNE'S WORLD AUTHORS SERIES (TWAS)

The purpose of TWAS is to survey the major writers —novelists, dramatists, historians, poets, philosophers, and critics—of the nations of the world. Among the national literatures covered are those of Australia, Canada, China, Eastern Europe, France, Germany, Greece, India, Italy, Japan, Latin America, New Zealand, Poland, Russia, Scandinavia, Spain, and the African nations, as well as Hebrew, Yiddish, and Latin Classical literatures. This survey is complemented by Twayne's United States Authors Series and English Authors Series.

The intent of each volume in these series is to present a critical-analytical study of the works of the writer; to include biographical and historical material that may be necessary for understanding, appreciation, and critical appraisal of the writer; and to present all material in clear, concise English—but not to vitiate the scholarly content of the work by doing so.

Ivan Goncharov

By ALEXANDRA LYNGSTAD
Fordham University
and
SVERRE LYNGSTAD
Newark College of Engineering

Twayne Publishers, Inc.　::　New York

To Karin and Janusz

Preface

In the English-speaking world Ivan Alexandrovich Goncharov (1812–91) is generally known as the author of one book, the great novel *Oblomov,* and whatever criticism has been forthcoming deals mainly with this work. Except for Janko Lavrin's brief study, *Goncharov* (1954), no comprehensive treatment of his fiction exists in English. This scanty, one-sided attention may partly be due to the lack of adequate translations. For example, the last of Goncharov's three novels, *The Precipice* (*Obryv,* 1869; also called *The Ravine* and *The Steep*), has never been properly translated into English, since the version put out in 1915 by Alfred A. Knopf was greatly abbreviated, and mutilated beyond recognition. His first novel, *A Common Story* (*Obyknovennaia istoriia,* 1847), has fared somewhat better. The Constance Garnett translation came out in New York in 1894 and was reissued in London in 1917. But forty years were to pass before a new translation (*The Same Old Story,* 1957) was made available by the Russians themselves. The only one of Goncharov's novels to which the English reader has had ready access during the last several decades is *Oblomov.*

In the Soviet Union, on the other hand, all of Goncharov's novels are popular classics. Though no collected edition appeared between 1916 and 1952, each work was frequently published separately. For example, in 1936 as many as five different *Oblomov*s were issued, along with one edition of *The Precipice* and two of *A Common Story*; in 1950 no less than four editions of *The Precipice* appeared. Since 1952 there have been three collected editions, as well as numerous reprintings of the individual novels. Truly surprising is the continued popularity of *The Precipice,* a work with a strong antinihilist bias and religious undertones. Between 1917 and 1964 it was reissued separately twenty-two times, eight more than *A Common Story*, which is generally considered to be "progressive" in tendency.

While Goncharov's literary reputation was early established and has remained relatively stable, scholarship on him was slow in getting under way, being seriously hampered by the scarcity of personal documents. The responsibility for this quandary, most acutely felt in studying the young Goncharov, rests squarely with the author. Shortly before his death, in an article entitled "Infringement of One's Will" (1889), Goncharov requested everyone in possession of his letters not to permit their publication and eventually to destroy them. Several correspondents, including some near kin, complied with his wish. Shortly afterwards, it is reported, Goncharov burnt his personal papers. Despite these handicaps, scholars have had considerable success in opening up the life of the cagey bachelor. With his *Un maître du roman russe: Ivan Gontcharov* (1914), still an invaluable scholarly resource, the Frenchman André Mazon became the first dean of Goncharov studies. Of comparable importance were the critical-biographical studies of E. A. Lyatsky, who, however, managed to complete only the first volume of his biography, *Roman i zhizn'* (Romance and Life, 1925); it ends with the year 1857. A definitive biography of Goncharov still remains to be written. An important preliminary appeared in 1960, "A Chronicle of I. A. Goncharov's Life and Work" (*Letopis' zhizni i tvorchestva I. A. Goncharova*) by A. D. Alekseev; this document provides a day-to-day record of the author's experience. A collected edition of the letters, hitherto available only in selections, is long overdue.

The criticism of Goncharov covers a wide spectrum of interpretation. During his lifetime he was generally viewed as a "critical realist" in the so-called Gogolian tradition, and his work was judged mostly by sociological criteria. Around the time of the author's death, Dmitry Merezhkovsky presented a counterbalancing view through his reinterpretation of much of Russian literature in the spirit of Symbolism.[1] By their emphasis upon the subjective, autobiographical elements in his novels, Mazon and Lyatsky indirectly justified this new direction. While Soviet scholars still stress the sociological "realism" of Goncharov, one critic, N. I. Prutskov in his "Goncharov's Art of the Novel"

(*Masterstvo Goncharova-romanista,* 1962), discusses symbols as an accepted part of his literary technique. A more balanced view of Goncharov, which does justice to all aspects of his work—psychological, social, and esthetic—seems to be taking form.

The present study will focus exclusively on Goncharov's achievement as a novelist. Therefore, his admirable travelogue, *The Frigate "Pallada"* (1858), will not be discussed, and reference will be made to his memoirs and critical essays only to the extent that they provide sidelights on his major fiction. However, we have offered a background psychological sketch of the author and a discussion of his literary apprenticeship. While our analysis of the individual novels does not conform to a uniform pattern, we have tried throughout to maintain a reasonable balance between the claims of theme and technique, the author's vision of life and its artistic expression. The final chapter, intended as a kind of synthesis, suggests the peculiar quality of Goncharov's talent and achievement.

Contents

Chronology

1812   Ivan Alexandrovich Goncharov, son of a prosperous grain merchant, born June 18th*, in Simbirsk (now Ulyanovsk) on the Volga.

1819   After father's death September 22nd, N. N. Tregubov, a retired naval officer, helps Mrs. Goncharov raise the children.

1820–   Attends boarding school near Simbirsk.
1822

1822   On July 20 sets out for Moscow to join elder brother, Nicholas, at School of Commerce.

1826–   Becomes seriously interested in literature; begins to write.
1827

1830   Leaves the School of Commerce without graduating.

1830–   Moscow University being closed because of cholera, Gon-
1831   charov spends year in Simbirsk.

1831–   Attends Moscow University as student of philology.
1834

1832   Excerpt of Goncharov's translation of Eugene Sue's romantic novel *Atar-Gull* appears in *The Telescope,* journal edited by N. I. Nadezhdin, one of Goncharov's professors.

1834–   Serves as secretary to governor of Simbirsk.
1835

1835   In May leaves for St. Petersburg and goes to work as translator in Foreign Trade Department of Ministry of Finance. In the summer begins to frequent the literary circle of Nikolay and Eugenia Maykov and to tutor two of their sons, Apollon and Valerian.

---

* The dates are indicated according to the New Style, conforming to the Western calendar. In the nineteenth century, the Julian calendar used in Russia ran twelve days behind its Western counterpart.

1836   Several poems by Goncharov appear in the Maykovs' private handwritten journal, "The Snowdrop" (*Podsnezhnik*).

1838   Story, "The Evil Sickness" ("Likhaia bolest'"), first printed in 1936, appears in "The Snowdrop."

1839   Story, "A Lucky Error" ("Schastlivaia oshibka"), appears in "Moonlit Nights" (*Lunnye nochi*), private miscellany of the Maykov circle.

1842   Writes physiological sketch, "Ivan Savich Podzhabrin."

1843   Begins novel, "The Old People" (*Stariki*). Later discontinued because of Goncharov's diffidence in his talent.

1846   In April meets the influential critic V. G. Belinsky; reads first part of A Common Story (*Obyknovennaia istoriia*) before his circle.

1847   A Common Story, written mainly in 1845, appears in the March and April issues of The Contemporary.

1848   "Ivan Savich Podzhabrin" appears in the January issue of The Contemporary. A Common Story comes out in book form.

1849   "Oblomov's Dream" (written in 1848) appears in illustrated collection of writings brought out by The Contemporary.

1851   Goncharov's mother dies April 23.

1852–   Serves as secretary to Admiral E. V. Putyatin on a world-
1854   wide sailing expedition undertaken chiefly to initiate trade relations with Japan. Expedition cut short because of outbreak of Crimean War.

1856–   Serves as censor in Ministry of the Interior.
1860

1858   Travel sketches, The Frigate "Pallada," published in book form.

1859   Oblomov appears in the January to April issues of Notes of the Fatherland. Published separately October 12. Goncharov accuses Turgenev of plagiarism (letter of April 9).

1860   In early April a group of mutual friends arbitrate in dispute between Turgenev and Goncharov, finding the coincidences between Goncharov's "program" for The Precipice and Turgenev's novels quite natural, since all had sprung from "one and the same Russian soil."

1862   From October 1862 to July of following year is editor-in-chief of the official newspaper, *The Northern Mail.*

1863–
1868   Serves as member of Board of the Press (from September 1865 Board of the Chief Directorate of the Press) in Ministry of Interior.

1864   Reconciles with Turgenev at funeral of critic A. V. Druzhinin (February 2).

1867   Receives Order of Vladimir (Third Class) for "outstanding and diligent" performance as a public servant.

1868   Retires January 10, evidently for reasons of health (impaired vision), with annual pension of 1750 rubles.

1869   From January to May *The Precipice* (*Obryv*) appears in *The Messenger of Europe* (*Vestnik Europy*).

1870   On February 3 *The Precipice* comes out in book form.

1872   On March 3 his critical essay on Griboedov's comedy *Woe from Wit,* "A Million Torments," appears in *The Messenger of Europe.*

1875–
1878   Writes *An Uncommon Story* (*Neobyknovennaia istoriia*), a secret memoir devoted mainly to proving his charge of plagiarism against Turgenev. Printed posthumously in 1924.

1879   Goncharov's article "Better Late Than Never," an extensive explanation of his literary intentions, appears in *Russian Speech.*

1880   Sketch, "A Literary Evening," appears in *Russian Speech.* In December, volume entitled *Four Sketches,* containing "A Literary Evening," "A Million Torments," "Notes on the Personality of Belinsky" and "Better Late Than Never," is published.

1883   In December his eye condition worsens; complete loss of sight in right eye. In same month his *Collected Works* published in eight volumes.

1886   Second edition of *Collected Works* appears.

1887   Reminiscence, "From My University Recollections," appears in *The Messenger of Europe.*

1888   Four character sketches, collectively entitled *Old-time Servants,* are published in the journal *The Field* (*Nivá*). *The Messenger of Europe* prints another recollection piece, "At Home" ("Na rodine").

1891   Dies September 27.

CHAPTER 1

The Man and the Mask

IVAN GONCHAROV was a man of many contradictions, concealing deep tensions under an impassive exterior. His "veiled" look and the nonchalantly-held cigar, both notable features of I. N. Kramskoy's well-known portrait of 1874, convey his dominant persona, which is also reflected in some of his writings. At the end of *Oblomov*, for example, Stolz is in the company of a writer, "a stout, apathetic-looking man with melancholy and, as it were, sleepy eyes."[1] Another self-portrait is given in "A Literary Evening" in the guise of the middle-aged writer Skudelnikov, who

sat in his armchair without stirring, as if he had grown onto it or had gone to sleep. From time to time he raised his apathetic eyes, glanced at the author and again lowered them. Evidently, he was indifferent to the reading as well as to literature itself—in general, to everything around him. (VII, 107)

But this man, outwardly so calm, at least in his self-image, was inwardly racked by frustrated ambition, professional jealousies, and all sorts of anxieties. A sedentary person who loved peace and quiet, at the age of forty he joined a sailing expedition bound for the ends of the earth. In a letter to Mr. and Mrs. M. A. Yazykov of September 4, 1852 he writes:

Everybody was surprised that I could resolve upon such a long and dangerous journey, lazy and spoiled as I am! If they knew me, they would not be surprised at this resolution. Sudden changes constitute my character; I am never the same two weeks in a row, and if I seem externally constant and true to my habits and inclinations, that is only because of the fixity of the forms in which my life is contained. (VIII, 248)

The tension between persona and inner self assumes concrete form through Goncharov's double professional allegiance. Timid and excessively modest about his literary talent, as well as fond of creature comforts, he does not seem to have seriously considered devoting himself exclusively to literature, but decided to make his living as a government official. However, the bureaucratic path was not an easy one; only after his extraordinary service on the *Pallada* did the promotions come quickly. In a reminiscing letter to his intimate friend and literary assistant Sofia Nikitenko, he speaks of a "school undergone for two decades with agonizing daily thoughts as to whether there would be firewood and boots when needed, or if the winter coat ordered on credit at the tailor's could be paid for."[2] But regardless of whether he was near the point of deprivation or well set up, whether he was locked in a subordinate position or moving quickly up the ranks, Goncharov always felt his service duties as a heavy burden. In 1874, more than six years after his retirement, he tells Countess A. A. Tolstoy: "I always wanted, and was called, to *write;* and meanwhile I was obliged to serve. . . . I always did what I did not know how to do or did not want to do." And he exclaims bitterly: "A whole lifetime in the service for a piece of bread."[3]

His situation assumes an ambiguous cast due to the fact that he, a literary man, for eight years served as a censor. The liberal critic A. V. Druzhinin comments on this appointment as follows:

I have heard . . . that Goncharov will go to work as a censor. One of the foremost Russian writers ought not to accept a position of that kind. I do not consider it a shameful one, but, first, it takes time away from the writer, secondly, it displeases public opinion, and thirdly . . . thirdly, a writer ought not to be a censor.[4]

Goncharov's experience was to justify Druzhinin's doubts. A letter of 1858 to P. V. Annenkov shows that his position as censor caused strain between him and his fellow writers and even was a source of social embarrassment (VIII, 303–4).

Goncharov gives a sociological explanation of his predicament, asserting that during his formative years literature was not yet considered as an organic part of culture in Russia. "With us," he writes to Miss Nikitenko in 1860,

> the literary man was not a plant that grew up on social soil, out of social needs; he was some sort of solitary, separate, accidental plant, a luxury and not at all a necessity and, moreover, a luxury long declared to be harmful, like tobacco in the old days. He was trampled on, crushed, exterminated—and he was almost always contraband.

A change came only with Gogol's time, he declares, when finally "people began to see in the belletrist something serious, necessary, and important." But by 1830, when he was reaching maturity, this had not yet come to pass, and he was therefore unable at the time to choose literature as his "duty" and his "calling" (VIII, 333). Though this may be nothing but the special pleading of a wretched man who felt artistically unfulfilled, the subjective point is worth noting: Goncharov was convinced that his failure to find his calling and develop his talent at the most opportune time was due to Russian backwardness.

His frustrations, however, may be partly traceable to his own social background. By birth Goncharov belonged to the merchant class (*kuptsy*), not especially famous for its cultural interests. Though his family was well above the average level of its class—referred to by the critic Dobrolyubov as the "dark kingdom"—when the time came to choose a school for Vanya, his widowed mother decided upon a mercantile education. The years spent at the Moscow School of Commerce were, in Goncharov's opinion, largely wasted. In his mid-fifties he could still, in a letter to his brother, write with rancor about his experience at the school, in which, he says,

> we moped around . . . for eight years, our best eight years, without anything to do. Yes, without anything to do. And, what is more, he [the principal] held me back for four years in a junior class, though I was better than everybody else, just because I was too young, i.e., too small. . . . He saw to it that it was quiet during the lessons, that we didn't make noise, that we didn't read anything unnecessary, what didn't belong to the lessons; but he wasn't smart enough to appraise and dismiss his dull and stupid teachers.[5]

He mentions several incompetent teachers by name and comments on the dry, unimaginative methods of instruction. Finally, at eighteen, Goncharov evidently convinced his mother during the summer holidays that a commercial career was not for him, and he left the school without graduating.

By its very mediocrity the School of Commerce may have deeply influenced the formation of Goncharov's character. During his last years there, A. Rybasov reports, the boy read a great many French romantic novels in the original, but "neither among the teachers nor his schoolmates did Goncharov meet a person who could teach him to examine what he read, to understand poetry, and to form his taste."[6] Actually, he had engaged in haphazard reading from a very early age, ever since he was sent to boarding school across the Volga in 1820. Within two years, the extent of his stay, he devoured every book in the small library, ranging from travel descriptions, history, and poetry to works by Voltaire, Rousseau, Sterne, and Mrs. Radcliffe—"in short, an inconceivable mixture." In his own judgment,

this indiscriminate reading, without supervision, without guidance and, of course, without any criticism or even any consecutive order, prematurely opened the boy's eyes to many things and inevitably speeded up the growth of his imagination, already too lively by nature. (VIII, 228)

This sustained habit of reading, at the School of Commerce chiefly a means of escape from a dull, humiliating reality, may have fostered a tendency to create a "special world," as young Aduev in *A Common Story* puts it.[7] Though as a university student Goncharov allegedly overcame his passion for French Romantic fiction by means of "English and German literature, as well as by acquaintance with ancient historians and poets" (225), "the exclusive concentration of bookish interests," Rybasov suggests, "created the possibility of a certain alienation from life, withdrawal into a world of lofty, but lifeless dreaming."[8] In any case, the evils of an excessively active fancy, as opposed to the demands of real life, were to become one of the major themes of Goncharov's fiction. In his life, as we have seen, the dualism was reversed: the "evil" necessity to work interfered with his creative imagination.

This creative imagination was an ambiguous gift; the adult Goncharov was haunted by the fear that it might fail him. In childhood his fantasy, that of a boy who "loved to hide in a corner and read everything he came across" (VII, 513), could rely on outside sources for stimulation; now he depended on his *own* imagination not only for personal happiness but also for artistic success. Significantly, Goncharov explains his manic-depressive moods in terms of the action or inaction of the imagination. Ennui, his greatest evil, is attributed to the exhaustion of the imagination, no longer able to sustain the ideal world. The analytical activity which replaces it is a double-edged sword; for though "analysis cuts through falsehood, darkness, and drives away the fog"—he writes to his friend I. I. Lkhovsky in 1858—it also discloses, "behind the fog, the abyss." Thus, ennui will always threaten, peeping out through "every gap between two pleasures, that is, every time the imagination has grown tired and keeps silent" (VIII, 300). This personal dilemma never ceased to supply themes for Goncharov's fiction and is dealt with on an elaborate scale through Raysky in *The Precipice*.

The almost Schopenhauerian role of the imagination, and of art, in Goncharov's thought may be related to a deep neurosis. His letters abound with references to spleen (*khandra*) and to various physical maladies. After his return from Japan in 1855 until the early 1870's Goncharov spent nearly every summer at European spas. Sometimes he seems to suspect the psychological nature of his condition. Writing from Marienbad to the Nikitenko sisters in 1860, he tells how the desire to write was interrupted by "dejection, heaviness, spleen—in short, by that sickness . . . for which, perhaps, other waters than those of Marienbad are necessary." Then he rationalizes his condition as due to "the inception of old age" (VIII, 340), a reason for creative sterility invoked as early as 1849, at the age of thirty-seven (246). In his correspondence these complaints are repeated *ad nauseam* with no apparent solution in sight.

Partly, at least, these were symptoms of incipient mental illness. The first serious outbreak of Goncharov's latent paranoia occurred in his late forties, at a time when he was unsuccessfully trying to complete his third novel, *The Precipice*. Leon Stilman implies that his illness had been contained as long as "new im-

pressions . . . [were] creatively reworked."[9] But now, with his
imagination in the doldrums, it erupted in a quite crass form:
on the publication of Turgenev's *On the Eve* (1860) Goncharov
repeated, in no uncertain terms, a charge made against his
colleague already the previous year, namely, that he had plagiarized the "program" for his own unfinished book. From this point
on, Turgenev and his associates—all of whom are discussed in
minute detail in *An Uncommon Story*[10]—provided the magic key
to all his misery and frustration. In that strange document he
systematized his feelings, erecting an intricate structure of self-
aggrandizement to soothe his lacerated ego. In the process, most
of Turgenev's longer fiction, Flaubert's *Madame Bovary* and
Sentimental Education, as well as several other European novels,
were reduced to echoes of his own work. This complex tissue of
fabrications betrays a profound sense of insecurity and inferior-
ity, feelings that in his last fifteen years became institutionalized,
so to speak, in a reclusive way of life.

His psychic malady, for which apparently he had a hereditary
predisposition,[11] clearly hampered Goncharov both in his natural
quest for love and happiness, and in his writing. Highly susceptible to women and frequently in love, he had little success in
his courtships and remained a bachelor all his life. His tendency
to treat passion intellectually, as a theme, may be related to this
situation. His problems are reflected in Alexander Aduev, Oblomov and Raysky, whose behavior at times is quite neurotic.
Their relationships with women are a source of great suffering;
they are extremely egocentric, often to the point of infantilism;
and while subject to extreme changes in mood, from the euphoric to the abysmally wretched, they are all afflicted with
ennui and can escape it only through the workings of fantasy.
And yet, with such unpromising heroes, molded from the stuff
of his own unhappy experience without his creative triumphs,
Goncharov is a great writer.

For the fictional world of which these neurotic heroes are a
part is eminently sane, rooted as it is in the life of the landed
gentry, still a dominant class in Russia. Goncharov acquired an
early familiarity with this class through his godfather, N. N.
Tregubov, a country squire who had settled permanently in
Simbirsk and lived in a wing at the Goncharovs'. After the death

of Ivan's father in 1819 he merged his household with that of Mrs. Goncharov. In consequence, her housekeeping was on a large scale, and their life differed little from that of the middle gentry. Much has been made of the resulting double class heritage, whereby the cultural aspirations of the gentry were engrafted upon the practical bourgeois ethos.[12] Potentially a source of conflict as well as of a broader humanity, this peculiarity of his social background helps to elucidate important aspects of Goncharov's work.

CHAPTER 2

Goncharov's Literary Apprenticeship

UNTIL the 1920's Goncharov's literary beginnings were largely unexplored, and his brilliant first novel, *A Common Story*, could only be seen as the product of a natural, untutored talent. While André Mazon discusses "A Lucky Error" in his book of 1914, this early story was made available only in 1920, in an appendix to the Stockholm edition of a critical study by E. A. Lyatsky.[1] In Russia it was first printed in 1927, with a foreword by Alexander Tseitlin.[2] Gradually, an extended apprenticeship, going back to the novelist's mid-teens, was uncovered. The fact that Goncharov had reached the age of thirty-five when he first was published, was partly due to lack of confidence in his talent, and partly to a highly exacting taste.

Nor was the literary scene during Goncharov's formative years conducive to promoting a quick and early focusing of literary ambitions. The 1830's form a transitional period in Russian literature. While producing romantically-inspired literature as varied as the historical novel, Lermontov's *mal du siècle* poetry, and Gogol's fantastic tales, these years also show—especially from 1835 on—a definite trend toward realism. This trend is manifest in several ways: in the growing importance of prose fiction, in the broadening base of literary subject matter and, despite the official nationalism sponsored by the Government, in the beginnings of a literature of social criticism.

The shift in public taste from poetry to prose is perhaps best shown by the fact that Pushkin, a "born" poet, from 1830 on devoted much time to prose composition. His *Tales of Belkin* (1831) significantly extended the domain of Russian letters, particularly through "The Station Master," the first successful portrayal of the "little man" in Russian fiction. Stylistically, the flair for parody demonstrated in this collection places it within the realistic trend. Though a decade and a half were yet to pass before the founding of the national school of Realism, pioneered by such leading figures of the Natural School as Dal, Sollogub, Butkov, and Gogol, the critical tendency associated with realism was already present. This tendency is traceable in such diverse writers as the fabulist Krylov—still active in the 1830's—the romantic Bestuzhev-Marlinsky, and N. F. Pavlov, author of *Three Tales* (1835), a work which sounds a clear note of social protest.

The simultaneous currency of several literary trends inevitably led to a mixture of styles. Thus, Pavlov presents the theme of "the insulted and the injured" in typical romantic manner, replete with unexpected twists of fortune, exceptional passions, and resounding rhetoric. Some of the early stories of Prince Vladimir Odoevsky show an even sharper contrast between theme and manner. In *Motley Stories* (1833), a critique of fashionable education takes the form of a gruesome allegory: a young girl has her heart torn out and her tongue twisted, after which she is consigned to a dress shop as a dummy. Though Goncharov was held back from stylistic vagaries of this kind by his conservative temperament and artistic tact, his early attempts to write show that, while trying to shape his own style, he was sensitive to the contending literary manners of the day.

Goncharov's introduction to the literary world came about in 1835, through his acquaintance with the family of Nikolay and Eugenia Maykov, whose two oldest sons, Apollon and Valerian, he subsequently tutored. For a person who, since the age of fourteen or fifteen, had read indiscriminately whatever he could lay his hands on and, without any notion that he had talent, had been writing "continually,"[3] the art-intoxicated atmosphere of the Maykovs' literary salon must have been exhilarating, indeed. The members of this family constituted a sort of miniature art colony. The elder Maykov was a famous academic painter, while his wife was a poetess and a writer of children's books; two of four sons who were later to have a literary career were already trying out their talents. The romantic idealism prevailing within the Maykov Circle was well suited to Goncharov, then a recent graduate of Moscow University, a seedbed of idealism, and somewhat of a romantic himself. The group's estheticism,

too, must have been agreeable to a person who, at a time when
Moscow University was being watched by government agents,
stayed aloof from the critical spirits among the students and met
neither Belinsky nor Herzen. In his university reminiscences,
written in the 1860's, Goncharov speaks about the "youthful
crowd" of students as a "little republic of learning over which
stretched an eternally blue sky, without clouds, without storm
and without internal shocks, and without any history except
universal and Russian history as taught from the rostrum" (VII,
203).

Deferring to the widespread contemporary view that poetry
was a sort of ticket of admission to the intellectual world (VIII,
75), Goncharov, like Gogol and Turgenev, began by trying his
hand at verse, imitating the artificial romantic manner of V. G.
Benediktov, a slightly older poet with whom he became intimate
in the Maykov salon.[4] The four poems we know, included in
three separate issues of the Maykovs' private journal "The Snowdrop" (*Podsnezhnik*) in 1836,[5] are pale exercises in lyrical reminiscence, thin in substance and conventionally elegiac in mood.
They are important to us mainly because eleven years later parts
of them turn up, slightly debased, in Goncharov's first novel.
His merciless self-parody in this instance climaxes a movement
away from romanticism which is already apparent in Goncharov's
first attempt at prose narrative.

I *"The Evil Sickness": An Exercise in Burlesque*

"The Evil Sickness" ("Likhaia bolest")[6] appeared in "The
Snowdrop" for April, 1838. It grew out of Goncharov's intimacy
with the Maykov family and is aimed at the romantic fads of
the author's best friends. Despite his low estimate of the story,[7]
it is of great interest for two reasons: it shows him in the process
of developing his comic manner, and it contains an early version
of the Oblomov type.

According to the mock equation at the basis of the story,
romanticism is a contagious disease requiring the serious attention of the medical profession. While not a physician, the narrator, a devoted friend of the afflicted Zurovs, assumes the mask
of a meticulous observer who is torn between his natural inertia

and a desire to save the sufferers. The chief symptom of the "evil sickness" is an inordinate lust for country hikes, a reference to the Maykovs' enthusiasm for the outdoors. Minor symptoms are "endless yawning, pensiveness, depression, lack of sleep and appetite, pallor and, at the same time, strange spots all over the face, and a queer wild gleam in the eye."[8] The recurrent yawning, a permanent motif in Goncharov's fiction, is particularly effective in focusing attention on the presumed pathological basis of the Zurovs' predicament.

The essence of the burlesque manner, here as elsewhere, consists in constant shifts from the sublime to the ridiculous. Coming upon a ravine, Mme Zurov calls it a "gloomy abyss" (35), whereupon Zinaida, a family friend, glimpses at the bottom of the ravine the skeletons of "sundry noble animals," soon identified as the bones of cats and dogs. The presentation of every object is determined by a sort of bifocal vision, which breaks up reality into opposed perspectives. Thus, a "still, smooth" lake is later said to be little more than a puddle, and a bridge across this so-called lake, constructed with "wonderful art and boldness" (32), allegedly has a pavement of dung. These are among the crudest examples of intentional bathos in the story; most shifts are more subtle and would require lengthier illustration. But whether subtle or crude, they embody the basic principles of Goncharov's developing comic style, one of maximum incongruity between a world perceived through romantic illusion and ordinary, sordid reality. Nature, with which the Zurovs wish to commune, is tainted with the evils of industry: in an earthly paradise where the birds in "harmonious choir sing a hymn of praise to the Creator," Nature's devotees nearly choke to death with the smoke and stench from a tallow-melting factory (33). This kind of style is familiar to any reader of satire. In view of Goncharov's modest experience at the time, his exercise in burlesque must be deemed quite successful. With the exception of a few lapses from good taste, he manages to maintain a light and airy tone throughout.

One is happy, nevertheless, for a modicum of character interest. In a story which may seem simplistic, Tyazhelenko, a corpulent landowner, is the redeeming nuance. Apart from his importance as a precursor to Oblomov—both conceal a lively

imagination and a warm heart beneath an apathetic exterior—
this figure introduces a sort of counterpoint into the story's
structure. Whereas the Zurovs are ever restless, flitting like
birds from one place to another and eventually "migrating"
abroad, Tyazhelenko, as his name—derived from *tiazhëlyi,* meaning "heavy"—suggests, is a veritable rock of stability, an embodiment of gross earthiness. Both in temperament and character he
is the direct opposite of the spiritually flatulent Zurovs. Known
since early youth for his "methodical laziness and his heroic indifference to the bustle of the world" (15), Tyazhelenko approaches a state of absolute equilibrium, being little more than
an extension of his bed. He gets up only for the main ritual of
the day, dinner, transacted in true Gargantuan style. While
producing a flourishing paunch, his manner of life is a cause of
grave concern to his doctors. It is this monument to obesity that,
in a long early conversation, opens the narrator's eyes to the true
condition of the Zurovs; at the same time he helps to project an
amusing contrast between a quiet life centered on food and a
dreamy enthusiasm for the outdoors.

It soon becomes apparent, however, that the Zurovs and their
inert friend are not related simply by contrast. For like the
afflicted family, Tyazhelenko is also repeatedly associated with
sickness. The narrator calls his laziness a "far more dangerous
sickness" than that which Tyazhelenko has diagnosed in the
nature lovers (18), and at another time he asks himself who is
sick, they or Tyazhelenko (25). The parallel is strengthened by
his being associated with Verenitsyn, a Byronic friend of the
Zurovs thought to be the source of the baneful infection; both
are referred to as friends of the family who "play an important
role in this business" (14). The parallel between the gross
Epicurean and the rapturous Romantics becomes even more
striking in view of their ends. In a brief epilogue the narrator
reports that, as predicted by his physicians, Tyazhelenko has
succumbed to a stroke, while the Zurovs, having left for America,
evidently perished on an excursion. At any rate, they never
returned. This ironic coincidence of opposites will turn up in
more subtle variations in Goncharov's later work.

One aspect of the story is untouched by the author's anti-
Romantic animus. Influenced, no doubt, by Pushkin's *Onegin*

manner, as well as by the narrative exuberance of Gogol's early stories and the idiosyncrasies of Laurence Sterne,[9] Goncharov utilizes a subjective mode of narration. He sets the scene through a prolonged series of reminiscences on the part of the narrator, followed by a humorous-sentimental allusion à la Sterne to his psychological state at the time of writing. His heart and mind, he confides, are too full for utterance; only after he has wiped his tears, which have overflowed onto the writing paper, is he able to go on with his story (11). The playful subjectivity of this narrative attitude agrees with the whole tone and tenor of "The Evil Sickness." However, in Goncharov's next story, much more serious in intent, the adoption of a subjective, at times even lyrical manner is partly responsible for its artistic failure.

II "A Lucky Error": A Mixture of Styles

Included in a private miscellany of the Maykovs, "Moonlit Nights" (*Lunnye nochi*, 1839), "A Lucky Error" ("Schastlivaia oshibka") belongs by genre to the stories of high society first practiced by Marlinsky and very popular in the 1830's. Obviously based on an anecdote—a young man is invited to a ball, but is by a "lucky error" brought to another—the story asks for the laconic treatment of Pushkin's *Tales of Belkin*. Instead, Goncharov's manner is early Gogolian, characterized by old-fashioned rhetoric, lyrical digressions, addresses to the reader, and apostrophes to his characters. The author's attitude toward his own created world is marked by an embarrassed archness which comes between the reader and the story.

The narrative begins with an elaborate passage of mood painting as twilight descends upon St. Petersburg, bringing a palpable change to every drawing room of the city. For a moment the decorous manners of high society relax their wonted rigor and passions emerge, to vanish once more as the candles are lit. This opening, oscillating between lyricism and humor, has little bearing upon the plot, which begins with a visit of young Egor Aduev, owner of three thousand serfs, to a good-natured but slightly spoiled society beauty of eighteen, whom he hopes to marry. The comic domestic vignettes that follow, technically motivated by Egor's observations as he wanders from room to

room in search of Helen, his lovely baroness, are even less
integral to the action. Of some importance, however, is a bit of
information about Egor, a world-weary man and a somewhat
jaded amorist who feels that his passion is the last sweet stirring
of a calloused heart and therefore his only hope for happiness.
This, together with his suspicion that Helen may be a coquette,
informs the situation with a minimum of dramatic interest.

The ensuing scene between the lovers comes off poorly for
several reasons. Generally it is too static, so that when the break
occurs it is not prepared for. The dialogue is stilted and the
psychology shallow. As we discover later, Helen has relapsed
into her cold, supercilious society manner, which Aduev reads
as a sign that she no longer loves him. This complication is
patently contrived: Aduev's lack of perspicacity is out of character for a man of his experience. As it turns out, however,
the Byronic Egor is a sham, the young man being no less callow
than his namesake Alexander Aduev, the future hero of Goncharov's first novel, for whom he seems to have been a study;
he also shares the latter's taste for romantic cliché.

A. Rybasov explains the divided image as follows: trying to
create a contemporary romantic type, Goncharov ended up imitating Griboedov and Pushkin. Consequently, Aduev is a syn-
thetic figure, part man of the world like Chatsky and Onegin,
part a naïve idealist like Lensky.[10] Rybasov's note goes to the
heart of Goncharov's failure in this story: he was still too overwhelmed by his predecessors to shape his own fictional world.

The complication is followed by a rather heavy-handed attempt at exposition, an element new to the society story, and by
two scenes showing the characters' reaction to their predicament.
Helen's unhappiness is set off against a sort of boudoir peep
show as she is being primped up for a ball, while Egor's frustration stands out from the way he acts the tyrannical master,
refusing every petition of his steward and viciously abusing his
old valet. Then we return to the plot as Aduev accidentally finds
a ticket of admission to a ball at the Commerce Club. The dénouement comes about through a mistake of the driver, who
takes him to a fancier ball at the Neapolitan Embassy, where,
again, he meets his beloved Helen. But before presenting the
reconciliation and betrothal the same evening, the author,

through Aduev, lovingly conveys the splendor and *bon ton* of the fashionable ambience. After Aduev returns home, the scenes with the steward and the valet are repeated with beneficent variations; ecstatic with happiness, the repentant master is ready to grant their every wish. It remains merely to enlighten Aduev and the reader concerning the "lucky error."

This lengthy summary was given chiefly because the story offers an insight into the creative laboratory of young Goncharov, who was clearly searching both for a subject and a style. Though his failure is due to several things, it lies mainly in his inability to fuse the compositional elements of the story into a coherent unity. Possibly because the conventional subject—a misunderstanding in love cleared up by a happy accident—did not really engage him, the author may have felt an unconscious need to give his story body through digressions from his theme. In any case, he devotes an inordinate amount of attention to atmosphere and *byt* ("way of life," morals and manners), presenting a number of sharply etched vignettes from several spheres of life. A second genuine ingredient in the story, though even less appropriate to the conventional *donnée* and the plot, is the psychological interest, manifesting itself, however awkwardly, in an attempt to explain the characters' predicament by their milieu and education. Unfortunately, since these characters are as stereotyped as the subject, the psychological analysis seems out of place. Add to all this the self-conscious narrative manner, with its excessive archness and obtrusive rhetoric, and we have an incongruous mixture indeed.

Stylistically, a similar confusion appears. The story shuttles back and forth between realism and conventional romanticism. On balance, it is the latter that wins out, although Egor Aduev is portrayed both with humor and irony. They are especially evident in Goncharov's treatment of Egor's righteous indignation at the peasants' petitions after his debacle. " 'Well, now I am calm,' he said, convulsively tearing at a button with one hand, while with the other he scratched his ear till it nearly bled— 'completely calm!' " After a passage which shows him recalling the "picture of his forfeited bliss," the same gestures are repeated more forcefully. "He tore off the button completely and scratched his ear all over till it bled" (VII, 459). Admittedly, this contains more than a hint of the comic-satiric manner developed with such zest in "The Evil Sickness." And yet, despite the ironic deflation of Aduev's emotionalism, a heavy residue of stereotyped romanticism remains both in the character portrayal and in other elements of the story. For example, the author's ridicule of Aduev's erotic utopianism, his Oblomovesque dream of marriage as a "poetic refuge" from "stupid neighbors, from the whole world" (450), does not prevent him from rejoicing in the sentimental success of his hero. Furthermore, the story embodies a motif of redemption of patently romantic provenience: the disillusioned Byronic hero, "to whom experience has . . . brought bitter fruits, mistrust toward people and an ironic outlook on life" (442), is saved through the love of a beautiful damsel. With such a highly charged psychological situation, no wonder that Goncharov's anti-Romantic tendency remained in abeyance and that his as yet unfocused striving toward realism could have little impact on his style.

III "Ivan Savich Podzhabrin": Realism Triumphant

In part, the limited success of "A Lucky Error" was due to its unrealistic genre. Significantly, Goncharov never again chose his heroes from the fashionable upper classes, but stayed within the confines of the provincial gentry and the middle ranks of the bureaucracy, circles which more readily lent themselves to realistic representation. His next story, the physiological sketch "Ivan Savich Podzhabrin," shows how much he gained thereby in terms of stylistic and structural unity. Though published only in 1848, this work was written in 1842, at the very time when the genre it exemplifies was being initiated by such men as Nekrasov, Grigorovich, Panaev, and Dal. In retrospect, Goncharov's decision not to publish the story at once seems to have been unwise, as it compares favorably to what other "physiologues" were turning out at the time. But whatever its literary value, as marking a stage in Goncharov's artistic development—his breakthrough to realism—"Podzhabrin" is of crucial significance.

A transitional literary form of the early and middle 1840's, the "physiological sketch" grew out of a desire to replace the stilted heroes, overblown passions, and unnatural language of the romantic story with true descriptions of actual life as conditioned by a particular locale and social milieu. Usually the object in these sketches is to depict the "physiology of life," the *byt* characteristic of certain urban groups, especially such as had hitherto remained outside the perimeter of literature. Most practitioners of the genre described life in the capital, St. Petersburg, and their characters range all the way from government clerks and lower-class intellectuals to organ-grinders and common drudges. A close Western counterpart to the Russian physiological sketch is Charles Dickens' *Sketches by Boz* (1836–37), which present life and manners among low-living Londoners as well as places of foregathering such as taverns, playhouses, and police courts. The Russian form, however, is both more humanitarian and more clearly a training ground for the realistic novel.[11]

Though "Ivan Savich Podzhabrin," subtitled "Sketches," has a larger format than most examples of its kind, it conforms quite nicely to type. The setting is a St. Petersburg tenement house, where Ivan Savich achieves notoriety for his unconscionable philandering. The action, consisting of a number of affairs, or attempts at such, between Ivan and four tenants—Anna Pavlovna, Masha, the "Baroness," and Praskovya Mikhailovna—is repetitive, yet varied because of the different social and occupational status of the women. The entire work is framed by a motif of moving; it begins with Ivan Savich looking for a new apartment because his neighbors are complaining about him, and it ends with a move in order to forestall catastrophe: being inveigled into a stupid marriage. No longer does Goncharov, as in "A Lucky Error," feel obliged to put together a plot, however perfunctory. Plot in the sense of a progressive sequence of events has disappeared, to be replaced by a simple rhythm of recurrence. This rhythm, which conforms to that of everyday life, has two advantages: it is realistic and it is comic. "Ivan Savich Podzhabrin" is a masterpiece of realistic comedy.

The basic pattern is that of a comedy of errors: except for Masha, the Baroness' maid, Ivan Savich's lady friends all turn out to be something else than they seem. Anna Pavlovna, who rents a few rooms across from him, soon becomes deliciously uninhibited and freely visits him. Every time she makes a nice remark about a rug, a chair, or some other piece of furniture,

he lets her take it to her own apartment. When the young man's
ardor has begun to simmer down, a middle-aged military man—
clearly her sugar-daddy—turns up, momentarily frightening Ivan
with the hint of an imminent challenge; but the danger evapo-
rates as the two men become friends over drinks. Next day,
however, Anna Pavlovna and her "uncle" are gone, along with
Podzhabrin's "sofa, table, clock, mirror, rug, two vases, a completely new tub, and a hammer" (VII, 36).

The sentimental loss to Ivan is minimal; he has lately been
"gaping at the windows of other apartments" (VII, 31), particularly that of the "Baroness." Discovering that a pretty girl ironing
across from his own apartment is this lady's maid, he dresses up
as a lackey and makes love to her. This is a patently hackneyed
device, but quite in character, and it does not reduce the story's
air of verisimilitude. When Ivan finally stands in the presence
of the Baroness, supposedly because he has his eye on her horse,
he finds a quite different person from pliable Anna Pavlovna:
she is lofty, cold, sophisticated. He becomes fired with the ambition to subdue this exquisite creature, who boasts counts and
princes among her friends. However, after being ill-used by
her—she refuses to acknowledge his loan of two thousand rubles,
not even his own money—and deeply insulted by her "friends"
at a wild party, Ivan must give up the Baroness, whom the
reader sizes up as a clever, unscrupulous courtesan.

The next affair, however, has already been prepared by a
chance meeting on the stairs. Indeed, the pattern throughout is
that of the round, the successive incidents being hooked onto
one another by partial overlapping. It is motivated psychologically by Ivan's curse of boredom and his attempts to escape it.
The new prospect, Praskovya Mikhailovna, is petit-bourgeois
and astringently virtuous. A regularly visiting godfather and a
dependent niece make for an unmistakable family setup, and
Ivan's discovery that he and the godfather have mutual friends
strengthens one's sense of encroachment: the tentacles are visibly
reaching out for the kill. The climax comes by way of a misunderstanding; for as soon as Ivan broaches the subject of love,
Praskovya interrupts him, thinking he is about to make a proposal. Not that she is unwilling, she simply needs time. A few
days later Ivan is astonished when the porter congratulates him,

intimating that his neighbors are busy preparing an engagement party. Panicky, he tells his valet to find another apartment at once and as usual absents himself for the day. For a moment the godfather contemplates suing, but gives it up because he has had trouble with the department in which Ivan serves. The story ends on an appropriately low note, with honor being replaced by honest appetite: "And they sat down to the table" (VII, 77).

The manner of "Podzhabrin" is that of the mature Goncharov, serene, unhurried, ironic. The battle with Romanticism may not be over, but it is suspended; so is his wrestling with psychology, which turned out none too well in "A Lucky Error." Instead, the author's burden of initiative seems to have been shifted over to the characters. A spirit of improvisation permeates the story, particularly the life of the title character, whose very existence, threatened by chronic boredom, depends on his ability to maintain a "questing" attitude in a drab world. Meanwhile the writer, having hit upon one of his great themes, boredom, gives the impression of effortless composition. The technical problems which beset him previously no longer arise, perhaps because they are solved indirectly and by the way, through the verve with which the central situation is apprehended. Consequently, the author appears not so much to create a world as to contemplate and describe one already in existence. He manifests himself as pure observer.

This is merely another way of saying that the author is in perfect control of his material, an impression that is confirmed by the fact that what he owes to others, a not inconsiderable amount, has been transformed and given his own imprint. Ivan Savich himself is undoubtedly inspired by Ivan Khlestakov, the gay adventurer and confidence man of Gogol's comedy *The Inspector General* (1836). Both Ivans are government clerks more noted for their zeal in the pursuit of pleasure than for devotion to the service. Prodigal sons of sorts, they squander their small independent fortunes on assorted vices: Khlestakov's greatest weakness is gambling, Podzhabrin's—women. But Khlestakov, too, cuts quite a figure as a ladies' man, having two affairs perking, with mother and daughter, before he stages his vanishing act. His boudoir chitchat is ever at the tip of his tongue: "How happy I am to be sitting by your side at last!" he coos, on first being introduced to the Mayor's wife.[12] Goncharov's Ivan makes love by the book, and the style of his formulaic wooing clearly owes something to Khlestakov. Furthermore, the latter mentions, besides "the fair sex," cigars as a weakness of his; the first thing we know about Podzhabrin is that he smokes cigars. These similarities suffice to establish an affinity between the two characters. Yet, Goncharov has in no way imitated Gogol. Whereas, for example, the burgeoning love intrigues in *The Inspector General* merely add a bitter-sweet excess to Gogol's comic-satiric theme, in "Podzhabrin" seduction is central. A ritual of lechery lays down the pattern of life for Ivan Savich, while Khlestakov is a nimble virtuoso of many vices. Even a detail like the cigars is used distinctively. For while in Gogol's comedy the cigars are just a part of Khlestakov's portrayal as a snob, in "Podzhabrin" they express the theme of ennui, as evidenced by the story's opening sentence: "Ivan Savich sat in his high-backed armchair smoking a cigar after dinner. To all appearance he was extremely bored" (VII, 7).

The main proof of Goncharov's originality, however, is his use of the main character. Apart from his intrinsic comic interest, Khlestakov is the vehicle of a collective epiphany, the gradual self-exposure of a provincial town. Podzhabrin's story may also expose the underlying mechanism of the life it touches, but the author's primary intent is a more modest one: to evoke in vivid detail the milieu of middle-class St. Petersburg. In doing so, he covers a broad social and moral spectrum, from the pseudo-elegant debaucheries of the *jeunesse dorée* frequenting the salon of the "Baroness" to the prickly petit-bourgeois respectability of Praskovya Mikhailovna. These extremes are pointedly contrasted through two parties, the Roman orgy at the courtesan's, where Ivan Savich is *de trop* and ends up in the role of scapegoat, and the Thursday family get-together at her successor's, where he is fêted as a man of the world. These ensemble scenes serve to depict two entire ways of life, from the characteristic style of the furnishings to related areas like manners and morals. For, actually, furniture is part of the moral picture in this story. With their showy elegance, the "huge chandelier," "mahogany sideboard," and cabinet for dainty tableware in the dining room of the "Baroness" (VII, 54) suggest a profound vulgarity under the surface glitter. The hard-core truth about virtuous Praskovya and her circle is similarly implicit in the quality of her dining room furniture, especially a sofa whose inviting appearance, inducing a sense of "quiet and comfort," is merely a front: when you try to sit on it, you rebound as from a rock: "So well were the springs made. . ." (69).

Ultimately, the individual milieus treated in the story intersect: the deceptiveness is general. "Loving" though she is, Anna Pavlovna is as mercenary as the "Baroness," with Praskovya not far behind: as soon as she finds out that Ivan Savich has an independent income, her virtue becomes less abrasive. Thus, a theme of acquisitiveness, of human feelings and relationships corrupted by money, pervades the story. In this connection, the order of the episodes is not coincidental; the sequence of kept woman, courtesan, and good girl is pointedly appropriate. Respectability comes to appear as hypocrisy, and the vivid portrayal of *byt* becomes a trenchant socio-psychological exposé.

Curiously, Goncharov balances these unflattering portraits with an almost sentimental presentation of real love in Masha, the Baroness' maid. This is no mere echo of Karamzin's saying in *Poor Liza* (1791) that "peasant girls too know how to love!" Masha is morally superior to the other women. Though as mercenary as the others at the outset, suffering not only fosters deep feeling, but activates her pride and sense of dignity. The author shows open sympathy for her as she cries "bitterly," contemptuously returns the money she has received from Ivan Savich, and begs him not to go to the Baroness' party. It is left to Avdey to console her. The valet's summing up of the situation sounds almost like an indictment: " 'These gentry think they are the only ones who have a heart,' he said, taking a sip from his glass, 'just because they drink liqueur!' " (VII, 53).

Such moments of pathos and potential criticism, however, are soon dispelled by the breezy realism of the tale; the many trifling details undercut emotion. Moreover, the characters have an air of farcical absurdity, especially incidental figures done in low relief. When a peasant in a sheepskin coat is asked whether he is the janitor, he merely yawns and looks away. Only at the fourth question, whether he is deaf, does he answer, "lazily":

"I'm not from here!" The janitor himself, sleeping through an awesome racket of repeated ringing and banging—a peasant knocked on his door until "the windowpanes rattled" (VII, 10)— later comments what a light sleeper he is. The enormous curiosity of the new neighbors as Avdey is moving his master's things is equally without rhyme or reason. These characters are not so much "humors" dominated by a single trait as eccentrics whose behavior, though habitual and true to life, is yet quite irrational.

Such vignettes of human unreason are more than isolated instances; they typify an absurd society of which Ivan Savich is very much a part.[13] Here is no agon between *alazon* and *eiron*, the old forms and the new vitality. The protagonist and the intended victims imply each other, as do Khlestakov and the townspeople in *The Inspector General;* indeed, Ivan Savich is more of a victim than his female opposites. His actions, certainly, are far less accountable than theirs, for neither lechery nor boredom can fully explain them. He is utterly devoid not only of a higher intelligence but of ordinary common sense, and finally must take flight to avoid entrapment. The sole counterpoise to this absurd society is offered by Avdey, who, unlike Zakhar in *Oblomov,* is more than a grotesque parody of his master. Avdey's role may be far from that of the "plain dealer," a sympathetic figure in ironic comedy who advocates a "moral norm,"[14] but he is all that Goncharov has seen fit to offer in the way of a norm. Avdey possesses not only intelligence and good judgment, but also a sense of honor. Whatever their faults, it is he and Masha, the servants, who ironically come closest to the human center in this story.

Technically and stylistically, "Podzhabrin" is executed with great tact and a fine ear for colloquial and fashionable speech. As fond of deliberate bathos as ever, Goncharov uses it less crudely than in "The Evil Sickness." The serial structure itself is built on bathos: despite his tender involvement, Ivan Savich sails on to the next affair with the zest of a Columbus in quest of the New World. The individual episodes tend to assume the same configuration, such as the menacing encounter with the sugar-daddy, Strekoza (meaning "dragonfly"), in which talk of wanting "satisfaction" dissolves under the mollifying influence of tea with cognac and Ivan Savich's cigars. The final scene, in which the godfather's thoughts of honorable revenge give way to his design upon the dainties meant for the engagement party, is true to pattern.

Goncharov's language displays an analogous characteristic through the intermingling of romantic and sentimental clichés with everyday speech. The handling of the rhetoric marks a distinct advance over "A Lucky Error," where the author's narrative is still tainted with stylistic stereotypes. In "Podzhabrin" the stereotypes are relegated to the dialogue. Thus the residues of second-hand romanticism have been objectified and now exist once removed from the author, forming a part of his subject matter alone. Liberated from solemn cliché, Goncharov uses it wonderfully for comic effect and to play up the contrast between appearance and reality. Anna Pavlovna, for example, is greatly addicted to pompous platitudes: among remarks about items of furniture, sofas, rugs, and mirrors upon which she turns a covetous eye, she scatters precious phrases about the "blows of fate" and being "destined for happiness" (VII, 30). When the sugar-daddy surprises their tête-à-tête, she becomes poetic in her despair: "What a storm-cloud has burst upon us. The dawn of our bliss is eclipsed" (33). Ivan, however, is quite a match for her in this sort of florid, pseudo-profound speech. Aside from his compulsive saying, " 'Life is short,' said one philosopher," he gets carried away occasionally by his own pretty sentiments. In a tender moment he tells Anna Pavlovna: "Tomorrow . . . I'll strew flowers on your life's way," to which she responds with: "And some nice pots from Poskochin's" (31). After her disappearance he reminisces to his drinking companions: "She was...how can I express it?...a sweet vision, a dream so to say...she brought variety to the tedium of a dead life" (37).

Despite Goncharov's low opinion of his early work, his apprenticeship to short fiction prepared him well for his subsequent endeavors as a novelist. His point of departure was the ethos and manner of romanticism, and he found his own style only through a struggle of exorcism which still left romanticism intact as a future subject. Stylistically, his early writings cover a wide range. While the characters and the plot of "A Lucky Error" are largely based on conventional romantic models, in "The Evil Sickness" the figures are drawn directly from life,

exemplifying what Goncharov later contemptuously called
"sketches"—*risunki* (VIII, 82). However, in "Ivan Savich
Podzhabrin" he transcended both local particularity and conventional stereotypes to create a type of character which embodied salient features of contemporary society. Podzhabrin, a
comic subspecies of the alienated man, is among other things
an expression of and protest against the "dead life" of Czarist
officialdom. The combination of individuality and the typical
here achieved is one of the most important manifestations of
realism in the story.

Goncharov's early stories have a special significance for his
first novel. Boris Engelhardt, pointing out that *A Common Story*
not only "makes use of the skills and devices worked out in the
writing of the stories, but also absorbs much of their content,"
calls them "preliminary studies" for this work. The monologues
of Alexander Aduev echo the "enraptured speeches" of the
Zurovs, the love scenes between Alexander and Nadenka go
back in part to "A Lucky Error," and a number of genre scenes
in the novel recall comparable scenes in "Podzhabrin."[15] For all
this, the novel represents a new level of achievement, far sur-
passing its predecessors in scope and complexity as well as in
seriousness of artistic purpose.

CHAPTER 3

A Common Story

G ONCHAROV'S first novel was a great success and, in the words of Belinsky, "produced a furor in St. Petersburg."[1] A later critic commented that *A Common Story* (*Obyknovennaia istoriia*) was to its time what *Fathers and Sons* was to be to a later period.[2] Formally, it is equally important. By 1847 a good many outstanding novels had appeared, exemplifying a wide variety of types such as the novel-in-verse (*Eugene Onegin*), the "frame-novel" composed of a cycle of stories (*A Hero of Our Time*), the "epic" novel (*Dead Souls*), and the epistolary novel (*Poor Folk*). Though notable achievements, each in its own way, from a formal standpoint these works are marginal, relying on the principles of other literary categories. Closer to the central norm of the modern novel, *A Common Story* stands at a turning point in the development of Russian fiction. From now on it is a steadily growing stream, with tributaries drawing upon most areas of Russian life.

The outline of the novel has a simple, archetypal quality reminiscent of a fairy tale: a young man of twenty leaves his placid country home to seek his fortune in the big city. But through this naïve fable Goncharov focuses on issues of prime importance to his contemporaries. The keynote is one of conflict between old and new, the provinces and the capital, country squire and industrialist-in-the-making—a dialectic that is reminiscent of the polarization between Westernists and Slavophiles. To Goncharov this struggle is ambiguous, and victory turns into a sort of defeat. For when the hero wins the princess, he is much tarnished. The fairy tale has become ironic, parodistic.

The opening scene, where Alexander Aduev is sent off to the capital, memorably describes the manner of life among the provincial gentry. The fussy mother with her endless advice about anything from almsgiving to sex; the hanger-on Anton Ivanych, a kind of comic "Wandering Jew" (I, 16); the pair of servants, Evsey and Agrafena, the latter with a tender heart beneath her shrewish manner—all these figures, though dissimilar in social standing, help to characterize the *byt* (mode of life) of the provinces. Its essence is an absolute belief in physical well-being; anything that threatens it is taboo. Such a creed not only fosters excessive pampering and emotionalism, but also breeds vice, as evidenced by the routine gluttony of an Anton Ivanych. To Alexander, this milieu must have acted as a sort of cocoon or womb, and the romantic idealism imbibed at the university does nothing to extricate him from it. Indeed, his academic dreams of love, friendship, and fame are merely another kind of sleep.

The rude awakening begins with Chapter II as Alexander meets his uncle, Peter Aduev, in St. Petersburg. The plot grows out of the ensuing conflict and is chiefly made up of Alexander's untoward adventures, interspersed with lengthy discussions between uncle and nephew. Peter, an inveterate city dweller who has not visited his provincial home since he left it seventeen years ago, is a utilitarian, well adapted to the cold, competitive, and lonely life of the capital. A successful official and manufacturer, he is initially a bachelor, but marries in the course of the story. With his nephew, however, his success is mediocre; despite repeated lessons in the uncle's pragmatic ethic, Alexander follows the will-o'-the-wisps of love, friendship and fame, and finds only disappointment. His colleagues in the office make friends to clean him out at cards, his beloved Nadenka "betrays" him, and his uncle has little faith in his verses. At the end of Part I, with the collapse of his love affair, Alexander is in a state of utter despondency: all his dreams have come to naught. At this juncture the aggressive uncle, whose star has been constantly rising, is suddenly caught short, his lessons in rational morality seeming beside the point. It falls to the lot of Lizaveta, his young wife, to bring Alexander out of the doldrums.

In Part II the author plays variations on the same themes, friendship, love and creativity, and yet avoids monotony. Goncharov is veritably Jamesian in the amount of "doing" to which he submits his subject. The first turn of the screw is applied to the theme of friendship, after Alexander meets his best friend, Pospelov, on Nevsky Prospect. But to his disappointment, this believer in eternal friendship who had "galloped over a hundred miles to say goodbye" when Alexander left for St. Petersburg some years ago (I, 21), takes their meeting very matter-of-factly and laughs at the other's hankering for "sincere effusions" (160). Alexander's always latent literary ambition fares no better when, encouraged by his aunt, he again turns to writing. Asked to judge the result, this time a novel, Peter—who believes his nephew should develop his proven ability as a translator and writer in the field of agriculture—offers no balm, but agrees to send it under his own name to an editor friend. The manuscript is returned, accompanied by a letter in which the editor, who realizes the uncle is just a front, indirectly accuses the author of "vanity, dreaminess, the precocious development of emotional predilections along with mental inertia, the inevitable consequence being idleness . . ." (179). After the manuscript has gone up in smoke, in a symbolic scene directed by Peter, the latter unintentionally launches Alexander on another love affair by asking him to cut out his business partner, Surkov, with Julia Tafaev, a young widow, because an affair might be harmful to their partnership. The ensuing romance, the longest episode in Part II, is an ironic parallel to the affair with Nadenka in Part I. For strangely enough, Julia, a languid voluptuary of the emotions whose romantic penchant for "sincere effusions" matches Alexander's own, soon wearies him; this time *he* becomes the betrayer. Feeling battered by life he tries to lose himself, withdrawing from society and mixing only with simple, uneducated people. The extent of his deterioration is shown by his treatment of Liza, a pure but passionate girl who comes his way while he is out fishing with the boys. Only a father's watchful eye prevents the seduction.

What option is left for such a man, a total failure in everything he has undertaken? Peter thinks he should go back to the country where he came from. And so he does. At the end of Part II, therefore, the book comes full circle, bringing us back to the patriarchal simplicities of the provinces. There, life has run its placid course; nothing has changed. But while the pastoral setting serves as a frame, it does not provide a set of values whereby the whole can be judged. True, Alexander's contact with his native soil and with his mother brings back revivifying memories of his childhood and youth and eventually cures his malaise, but soon he becomes bored and yearns once more for St. Petersburg. The book proper ends with two letters, one each to his aunt and uncle, in which he informs them of his speedy return to the city. In these letters, especially the one to his aunt, speaks a person who has reached the "time of consciousness" (I, 293), without losing his capacity for feeling.

The epilogue, in which the characters are shown four years later, gives a distinct hourglass shape to the work. The success of Alexander is complete as, balding and potbellied, he is about to wed a young heiress: "career and fortune" (I, 314).[3] Peter, on the other hand, is visibly declining, racked by rheumatism and anxious about the condition of his wife, who in the meantime has lost all zest for life. Pressured by circumstance, he is cutting short his career at the very moment when the younger generation is coming into its own. This ending suggests a round, an impression that is strengthened by Peter's forced admission that he, too, was once a dreamer. Uncle and nephew seemingly merge, and it looks as if maturing is to be equated with shedding of one's illusions and adjusting to life as it is.

I   A Common Story *and the Age*

Goncharov's first novel is closely related to its time, and a brief comment on the contemporary intellectual climate may help to elucidate its meaning. During the 1840's Romanticism was still an important force, and some of the leading thinkers, such as Herzen and Belinsky, severely criticized what they considered to be an obsolete view of life. Among Herzen's articles one is worthy of note, namely, "Romantic Dilettantes,"[4] which appeared in *Notes of the Fatherland* in 1843.

Belinsky's campaign against Romanticism provides specific parallels to Goncharov's novel. In "Russian Literature in 1842" he contrasts two extreme types of men, one utterly devoid of "soul and heart" as of ideal aspirations, the other being its diametrical opposite.[5] This contrast is further developed in "St.

Petersburg and Moscow," Belinsky's contribution to Nekrasov's collection *The Physiology of St. Petersburg* (*Fiziologiia Peterburga*), published in the spring of 1845 while Goncharov was at work on his book. Considering these types of men the "classical ones of our time," Belinsky comments: "Not belonging to either of them, we see something in the latter [the practical type], while as for the first—sorry—we see absolutely nothing."[6] In an earlier article, displaying similarities with Goncharov's novel both in thought and imagery, the critic gives a contemptuous description of the *schöne Seele*, Alexander's spiritual prototype. These "beautiful souls" recognize the "sublime and the beautiful" in a book, he writes, but lack "all sense of reality"; consequently, whatever they undertake they quickly "get *disillusioned* (their favorite word!) [and] their spirit grows cold. . . ." In the end they either "get reconciled to reality whatever it is like, that is, they fall from the clouds straight into the mire [*griaz'*], or they become mystics, misanthropes, lunatics, or somnambulists."[7]

Though similar in tendency, Goncharov's own view of the novel as reported some thirty years afterwards in *Better Late Than Never*, takes the "practical" type much more seriously. He writes:

. . . the meeting between the soft nephew, a dreamer spoiled by idleness and gentility, and the practical uncle gave a hint of a theme which had barely begun to emerge even in the busiest place of all, St. Petersburg. This theme was a faint glimmering of the consciousness that *labor*—real and not routine, but *active work*—was necessary in the struggle against the general stagnation of Russia.

In reference to the "concepts and mores" represented by the nephew, he says: "All that was becoming obsolete and was passing away, while faint gleams of a new dawn, of something sober, business-like and necessary were appearing" (VIII, 73). Peter is clearly conceived as an emerging type, one that embodies a new sense of life and a new ethic, while Alexander, the Schillerian romantic,[8] represents a type on its way out.

In a modified form, Soviet critics have extended this view toward a full-fledged sociological interpretation of the novel. In his introduction to Goncharov's *Collected Works* (1952–55),

S. M. Petrov sees the Aduevs as representatives of two distinct social classes, one in the process of deterioration, the other just forming. Stripped of its veils, the pseudo-romanticism of Alexander allegedly reveals the "egoism, self-admiration, and unfitness for life" of the serfdom-based gentry, while the pragmatism of Peter, the official turned entrepreneur, represents the no less egoistic and individualistic *Weltanschauung* of the rising bourgeoisie (I, xv). The ideal term within the dialectic triad is Lizaveta, who as the only truly positive character embodies, in Petrov's words, "the progressive idea of asserting women's right to happiness, to an independent spiritual life, an idea which is as much antiserfdom as antibourgeois" (xvi).

While plausible on the face of it, Petrov's assumption of a distinct class basis in Goncharov's treatment of his characters is scarcely tenable. Both the Aduevs come from the gentry, a fact which suggests that their dissimilar reactions to metropolitan life are due chiefly to differences in temperament. Despite a sociological bias in Goncharov's own critical pronouncements, his typology is more psychological than social.[9] He chose as the province of his art a limited sphere, loosely defined as that of personal relations, with society as a rather abstract entity felt mainly as the "spirit of the time." This "spirit" is incarnate in St. Petersburg life, which Alexander is unable to cope with—until the Epilogue. The book dramatizes the terrible cost of his success. To his aunt's wish to turn back the clock to four years ago when, as she says, he was "beautiful, noble, wise," he can only answer: "It's the age. I'm keeping up with the times—you can't lag behind!" (I, 312) Lizaveta's nostalgia suggests that it is the characters' purely human substance, not their class traits, which finds expression in the dialectic triad noted by Petrov.

By following the movement within this triad, partly precipitated by the tendency of the age, partly by Goncharov's subliminal humanism, the reader arrives at a true assessment of the novel's meaning. Initially his sympathies are all with Alexander, but in the course of the action they shift to Peter, an impressive figure of wide learning, high social standing and, seemingly, fine culture. Subsequently he, too, is undercut, leaving the aunt as the only character who has the author's full approval. Thus the novel creates a series of shifting moral perspectives or, to change the figure, a group of reflectors with unequal capacity for projecting the human image.

II *Ironic Form in* A Common Story

The tension between reality and appearance revealed by this play of perspectives is an indication of the basically ironic form of the book. Irony not only marks its narrative manner, placing a cool distance between the author and the paragons of success he portrays; it also informs the portrayal of character and the deployment of the action.

The ironic pattern takes definite shape as we watch Alexander and Peter turn into puppets of circumstance, false philosophy, and the vagaries of time. Despite his self-assurance, Peter is progressively overwhelmed by those forces which his pragmatic outlook has ignored. Having repressed his own feelings, he cannot understand the emotions he despises, so that, when he asks his relative to do him a good turn (cutting out Surkov with Mme. Tafaev), he causes human complications he has failed to foresee. This is a strange quandary for a man who preaches a prudential ethic, according to which an act is judged as good or bad by its consequences. When, eventually, Peter begins to speak "extravagantly," trying to bring Alexander back to his favorite ideas, the latter simply suggests a cigar, an emblem of his uncle's mercantile mind (I, 227). But spurn materialism as he may, Alexander gradually succumbs to it. Having seen through the petty mechanism of life, the lofty idealist turns into an inverted hermit, trying to "kill the spiritual principle in himself" (233). In the end he becomes a mockery of his former self and a "fat, bald, and rosy" (307) copy of the man whose values he once despised. In Merezhkovsky's apt phrase, his life is a "tragedy of banality."[10]

The Epilogue clinches the ironies of the story. The picture of Alexander—a former champion of abused child-brides against the ogre of an elderly husband—holding the trembling hand of his fiancée in his own without the slightest feeling, is sardonic. This is Hegel's "reconciliation with reality" with a vengeance. Peter's situation, that of a highly successful official who, to save his wife, chooses retirement at fifty to cultivate precisely those

illusions which he has persistently ridiculed, is fraught with unmistakable comic irony. The erring ways of reason always seem
more comic, perhaps because more avoidable, than the inexorable attrition of the feelings. But both characters are adept at
self-deception: having found their ambition, they carry it to
such a fanatical extreme that their humanity is fatally damaged.

III   The Fall of a Romantic

Despite being doomed by the tendency of the age, Alexander
is portrayed with considerable sympathy, with the result that
his story is riddled with ambiguity. It is impossible not to pity
the young man who, with the equivalent of a college education,
is by upbringing and experience completely unprepared for "the
struggle with what was in store for him, as for everyone." On
the other hand, Peter makes such exquisite fun of his naïveté,
his spontaneity, his lofty dreams of a "mighty passion" (I, 11) and
other attainments that Alexander begins to look ridiculous. As
late survivals of Romantic stereotypes, such ideas as eternal love
and friendship, along with divine inspiration, were highly vulnerable to ridicule, and A Common Story exploits this vulnerability to the limit. Ridiculed, too, are the sentimental clichés with
which Alexander's speech abounds, such as "sacred fire," "sincere
effusions," "cup of happiness," and the like. Possibly because of
his preference for "lofty" language and ideas, the curve of his
experience is a descending one, conveyed graphically through
a cluster of related images, mainly those of flight and fall.

A prodigal son rather than a hero of his time, Alexander sets
out for those "foreign parts" (I, 13) so much dreaded by his
mother to "try his wings" (20), to quote Anton Ivanych. And he
does his best; at least his uncle finds him ever "soaring" or being
"carried away" by something or other, whether on the "wings"
of poetry or love. The young man believes that as a poet inspired
from on high he stands far above the common crowd. Sometimes
his "high" intent assumes concrete physical expression. Crossing
the river to Nadya's home, for example, he acts like a man who
is only vaguely aware of gravity (86). The author invariably
accompanies these aspiring impulses with a mocking counter-

point, hinting at the inevitable fall. Consequently, Goncharov's double-edged style, oscillating between pathos and burlesque, acquires its full significance only within the framework of the imagery of flight and fall that shapes the novel's action. This imagery is so closely enmeshed in the book's texture that it makes even common clichés come alive, as when Nadya's threat to "tell mother" at a moment when he is still transported by his first kiss, causes Alexander to fall "from the clouds" (96). Indeed, the entire action seems to enact a single metaphorical idiom, namely, *popast' v omut* (to "get into trouble"), which literally means to fall into a slough, swamp, or pit. Variations are provided by expressions with *tina* (mire) and *griaz'* (mud). Some permutations of this dominant image will be examined, starting with expressions based on *omut*.

At the outset the mother, warning her son about the imminent venture, voices fear that he may be in for trouble, literally "get stuck in a swamp" (I, 10). Her fear is justified when, in his dejection, Alexander can see no way out of "the slough of . . . [his] doubts" (230). When his aunt tries to awaken him from his torpor, he tells her: "I would go to sleep for good, and here you arouse my mind and heart only to push them once more into the whirlpool" (256). "Whirlpool" brings out an additional connotation of *omut,* one which is more fully exploited later. According to Dal's dictionary this word originally denoted the pit under the mill wheel, a favorite haunt of malevolent water sprites; but these demons also used to sit in depressions in lakes and rivers, another meaning of *omut.* A moment before Alexander's return his mother tells Anton Ivanych a strange dream. In the dream Alexander comes to say goodbye to her for ever. When she asks him where he comes from, he points to the lake and says: "Out of the pit[11] . . . from the water sprites" (272). The motif is repeated twice by the mother, who from Evsey's and Alexander's reports on life in the capital has concluded that her dream was true. To her, evidently, only the word *omut* can describe a condition in which people wear themselves out with work, do not go to church, make love before they wed, and "betray" each other (280, 286). Yet, after one and a half years of a placid country existence, Alexan-

der "yearned to go back to the now familiar swamp" (291).
The fact that St. Petersburg was built on marshland playfully
extends the range of the idiom.

The association of *omut* with the lake sets up a connection
with *tina*, meaning "mud," "slime," "ooze" and, figuratively,
"mire." The first context in which this word appears makes it ex-
pressive of the idea of "naked" reality. Carried away by his own
rhetoric, Alexander compares life to a "beautiful smooth lake."
Like a lake, he says, it is "full of something mysterious and alluring, concealing so much—" whereupon the uncle rudely breaks
in, "Mud, my friend" (I, 52–53). The lake and the yellow
flowers that grow in it stand for idealized love of the sort dreamt
of by Alexander's maiden aunt. His own use of "lake" as an
image of life shows his romantic tendencies not only because
it is an idyllic piece of nature, but also because a lake can act
as a mirror, a romantic symbol of self-communion. Through
these juxtaposed images, namely, the smooth, reflecting surface
and the dark, turbid depths of the lake, two distinct views of
reality are epitomized. Though Goncharov seems to favor the
view of the uncle, other uses of *tina* suggest a different attitude.
For example, after the near seduction of Liza, Alexander's soul
once more "got sunk in the mire [*v tine*] of petty ideas and
material cares. But fate was not slumbering and he did not
manage utterly to perish [lit., "drown"] in this mire" (251).
It may be significant that *tina* is here, among other things, an
image of materialism, which is the creed of Peter Aduev. In
any case, Alexander falls through the "beautiful" surface and,
while getting a taste of the mud, also becomes acquainted with
the water demons—quite an accomplishment for someone who
was setting out for the Promised Land (10). Peter, incidentally,
is several times referred to as a demon. At one time Alexander
asks himself: "Isn't he a demon sent me by fate?" (101)

The vertical imagery, ranging from heaven to hell in a seemingly Manichean universe, is too intense to be mere comic hyper-
bole. One senses at the source of it the author's own feeling and
experience, magnified, to be sure, by a lively imagination. Alexander sees people as "wallowing in filth" (*griaz*, I, 163; also
"dirt," "mud") and his "sacred, exalted" feelings are "trampled

in the mud" (147); even his government job and his work as a journalist are referred to by the same term (101). Interestingly, Goncharov uses similar expressions in describing his own life experience, particularly in a letter to Sofia Nikitenko of June 20, 1860. Having reminded her of "all the coarseness and filth [*griaz'*] which hides in our Oblomovkas, in the midst of our official and private institutions, and in the emptiness and depravity of social life," he goes on: "If . . . you'd got immersed in this swamp [*boloto*] as I did, you . . . would perhaps wonder that I did not utterly perish" (lit. "drown"). Envisaging his past as a long "struggle with life" in the name of an "indestructible idealistic philosophy," he asks her to imagine a situation of "incessant falling" (VIII, 332–33). In *Better Late Than Never* Goncharov openly admits his closeness to Alexander:

When writing A *Common Story* I naturally had in mind myself and many like myself who received their education either at home or at a university, lived in a backwater beneath the wings of a good mother, and then were torn away from their blissful condition, from hearth and home, and sent off with tears (as in the first chapters of A *Common Story*), to appear next on the main field of action, St. Petersburg. (73)

Thus, while Goncharov may disapprove of Alexander's conduct, he deeply sympathizes with his sufferings, springing as they do from the defeat of the ideal in a bitter conflict between body and spirit, capacity and aspiration. He also sympathizes with his desire for happiness, as evidenced by his description of the St. Petersburg night which envelops a sweet moment in Alexander's romance with Nadenka:

How irresistibly everything disposed the mind to dreams, the heart to those rare sensations which in the light of regular austere everyday life appear such senseless, misplaced, and absurd digressions. Useless, to be sure; and yet it is only in such moments that the soul vaguely perceives the possibility of that happiness so strenuously sought and not found at other times. (I, 95)

Moreover, no satisfactory alternative is offered in the novel, the moralism of the uncle being woefully uninspiring.

IV A *Rationalist's Debacle*

At first glance, Peter Aduev seems not only intelligent, but likable. His personal aplomb, ready wit, and adroit handling of his nephew are both impressive and entertaining. His debunking of antiquated rhetoric and pretentious emotions is laudable, and even his utilitarianism fulfils a need of the age. Discussing Peter's role in *Better Late Than Never,* Goncharov speaks with evident admiration of his own character, who in becoming a factory owner allegedly took a daring step for an official of his rank.[12] Besides, he gave him some of his own pet ideas. A permanent ingredient in Goncharov's fiction is a counterpassion theme, and in *A Common Story* Peter is its chief vehicle. To the latter, passion is an illness. His dislike of excessive emotionalism is quite in keeping with the timely, socially-oriented ethos of work which he embodies, and in both respects he seems to have his creator's approval.

And yet, what a frightful bore Peter turns out to be eventually. While we may smile at Alexander's naïve deification of impulse, Peter's worship of reason, in a narrow pragmatic sense, is depressing and dehumanizing. The ultimate goals are taken for granted, his priorities being determined by the omnipotent spirit of the age. Though clearly not intended as such, Peter comes to look very much like an ironic reflection of Hegelianism. "For Hegel," we are told, "the only significance of the empirical history which we experience and in which we act lies in its embodiment of the necessary, dialectical movement of the Absolute Spirit." What option is there for man within such a perspective? ". . . must we not let history carry us along with it?"[13] Clearly, the individual becomes a medium for the dictates of the age.

And so, whereas Alexander's ethics are centered on the ego, Peter's are socio-centered, predicated on doing what the *Zeitgeist* demands. At the behest of the age Peter turns himself into a tool for accomplishing work; he lives for work and money, his Epicurean liking for comfort being just an ornament. What he really values are the things that momentarily are most highly prized by society: rank and financial success. And to accomplish these goals he treats both himself and others as objects. This is best shown in the Surkov affair, where he makes a convenience of Alexander. His wife is a permanent convenience, necessary for his complete success. To ensure her loyalty within their passionless marriage, Peter works out a system of psychological control.[14] Thus, the "progressive" antagonist turns out to be a systematic upholder of the status quo, a result quite in keeping with Hegelian premises.

By his manipulation of other people Peter causes great damage. A thoroughgoing rationalist, he considers right action possible only if based on a clear analytical understanding of one's motives and on the ability to predict the consequences of one's behavior. Applying these principles from the outside to Alexander, he unintentionally puts him in the position of a guinea pig, depersonalizing him in the process. In their long discussions, Peter picks his nephew to pieces, exposing his "true" motives and plotting the course of his conduct. Only half-humorously, he explains love in terms of Leyden jars (I, 13) and tells him lovers have changed very little since Adam and Eve. Scientifically correct perhaps, he is morally wrong. For this view turns Alexander, up to now proof against becoming a manifestation of the age, into a puppet of the ages: he becomes an illustration of a general human predicament. Thus, both he and Nadenka are reduced to anonymity, an idea that is reinforced by a frequent motif: "What's her name?" Nearly a score of these appear in the text, with different names for the girl. Whatever Nadenka does, even when she "betrays" him, is viewed by the uncle as "in the order of things," with the result, Alexander says, that "at twenty-five I lost confidence in happiness and in life and my soul grew old" (261).

The theme of changing human nature through science was a common subject for allegory in nineteenth-century fiction; the results of such experiments were usually shown to be disastrous. Examples of this theme in American literature can be found in Hawthorne's stories "Rappaccini's Daughter" and "The Birthmark." Though written in an entirely different style, *A Common Story* treats the same theme, since Peter aims at nothing less than to work a complete change in Alexander's nature (I, 259). Without being strictly scientific, his analytical method has the same provenience as the method of the scientist. In Alexander's case the result is not death, as in Hawthorne's stories, but inner division and dehumanization. He tells his uncle: "You evoked a struggle in me between two different views of life and you were unable to reconcile them. And what was the result? Everything in me turned to doubt, to a kind of chaos" (259–60). More specifically, Alexander was alienated from his own immediate experience, having become excessively aware of its causes and processes. For example, he started to analyze love, he says, "the way a student dissects a corpse under the guidance of a professor, seeing instead of the beauty of forms only muscles, nerves" (261). Not only, then, did the reeducation fail, but it introduced into the subject a foreign body which poisoned his system and vitiated his relationships with others.

Peter is shown up most thoroughly through his marriage. Upholding "rational" love against his nephew's insistence on mutual feeling (I, 75), he is at the end a sort of involuntary jailer to his own wife, who has lost not only her good health but her desire for freedom. She has been forced into a straightjacket of routine and conformity and can only echo the petty concerns of her husband. A perfect Philistine by now, Peter is too far gone to change his ways, and his belated efforts to make a new start are quite comic. Though impotent to assert herself, Lizaveta is morally superior to both men, combining an awareness of the claims of the heart with a fine intelligence. Therefore, her nostalgic vision of what might have been can still serve as an ideal norm whereby the two men are judged and found wanting.

V   Tertium quid: *The Reconciling Vision*

Women often function as touchstones in literature. This is particularly true for Russian fiction, where failure to win a woman's approval often spells decline or doom. In Dostoevsky, characters as diametrically opposed as Svidrigaylov in *Crime and Punishment* and Myshkin in *The Idiot* founder on this rock; rejected by Dunya, the former kills himself, while the latter, unable to meet Aglaya's demand for a full human love, ultimately collapses under the pressures of life. Goncharov employs women in this capacity in every one of his three novels. Oblomov understands he is damned when Olga leaves him, and in *The Precipice* Vera's rejection of both Raysky and Volokhov, together with her deepening feeling of friendship for Tushin, is a barometer of Goncharov's relative estimate of the three characters. In *A Common Story* Lizaveta performs the same function in regard to both husband and nephew.

What raises Lizaveta above both men is her broad humanity, harmoniously balanced between the conflicting demands of head and heart, reality and dream, self and society. In discussing Alexander with her husband, she says that "his mind is not on a level with his heart, and so he is to blame in the eyes of those whose minds have run too far ahead and who want to succeed everywhere by dint of reason alone" (I, 157). In her relationship with Alexander she wisely refrains from direct advice or criticism, knowing that he gets enough of that from her husband. After the collapse of his romance with Nadya she leaves it to her husband to show off his post-mortem wisdom, while she simply shares Alexander's suffering; afterwards "she returned to her bedroom with tear-stained eyes" (146). As skeptical of her nephew's literary talent as her husband, she knows that man cannot live without hope and tempers the reality principle with illusion. Therefore, after his other ventures have failed she encourages Alexander to take up writing again. Her interests also embrace society; she wonders, for example, whether Peter's unceasing labors are undertaken only "for petty reasons," such as the desire to "attain importance among men due to rank and wealth," or for a "common human aim" (150). But despite her clear vision, warm heart and good judgment, Lizaveta must perish, a victim of psychological tyranny.

She must perish partly because of the kind of novel Goncharov was writing, a double-edged comic exposure of two modes of life and two sets of values. In satire, particularly of the moral-philosophical kind, there is often a great deal of suffering, even death, without compensatory catharsis. Not to speak of the horrors of *Candide* (1759), there is the suicide of the Savage in *Brave New World* (1931), and a contemporary work like Dickens' *Hard Times* (1855) ends with a slew of disasters. When Gradgrind sees his daughter, Louisa, "the pride of his heart and the triumph of his system, lying, an insensible heap, at his feet" at the end of the second book of Dickens' hard-hitting novel,[15] he experiences the collapse of his entire philosophy of life. Similarly, Peter Aduev, about to be made a privy councilor, breaks out in a "cold sweat" (I, 304) at his impotence before the fateful consequences of his "system's" success. It is characteristic of the mid-nineteenth century that in both instances utilitarianism is the target of attack. Whether artistically justified or not, such strategic use of characters as vehicles of exposure is very effective in criticizing an ideology, if not in projecting a valid criticism of life.

VI *Character Portrayal in* A Common Story

It is quite in keeping with the qualities of satirical comedy that Goncharov's major characters in *A Common Story* should be intellectually conceived and sometimes act like disembodied abstractions rather than as semblances of real people. Conversely, those figures are most real who are least essential for implementing the theme. Not having to be at the author's beck and call, they are free to be themselves, to express their full esthetic potentiality.

Artistically weakest is Peter, on whom, ideologically, the novel turns, but Alexander, too, shows traces of abstraction. Convincingly to act the eternal "country bumpkin" untouched by his college education and city experience is not easy, and actually the young man is completely natural only in his native habitat. The formula for Alexander's behavior is similar to that for any *ingénu* figure and, as always, delightful situation comedy results from his inability to learn from experience. The opening scene in St. Petersburg, during which he nearly impales himself on his uncle's razor several times in succession in the attempt to embrace him, comes immediately to mind. However, such effects can be overdone, as happens when, regardless of Peter's murderous criticism of his poetry, Alexander holds out a sheaf of translations from Schiller and offers to make a "table of contents for all his articles in chronological order" (I, 58). This is perilously close to caricature. The *idea* of Alexander, of a person living in his own "special world," takes precedence over verisimilitude. Even worse, glaring inconsistencies arise from the different satirical functions he is called upon to fulfil. While

Alexander shows both insight and wit when the author uses him to expose the inanity of office work (59–60), the dull uniformity of young ladies (65), or the atrocious marriage practices that prevail in society (77–79), at other times he is degraded to the level of a fool, as when the young man calls a ring and a lock of hair "material signs . . . of immaterial relations" (45) or, after more than two years in the capital, behaves so childishly with Nadya.

Against the all-too-evident concept of Alexander, the real person comes through best in the abortive romance with Liza, an episode from daily life turned into a gem of youthful pathos. Here he is no longer one-dimensional: though he speaks like a mentor to Liza, he is constantly aware of her sexually; all along there is an obscure conflict between moral will and lust. Along with the later rustic Alexander, who is reminiscent of Oblomov, this agonized individual contains the core of a living character, a quality lacking not only in the country bumpkin but also in the rosy, balding man with a paunch who is put through his paces in the Epilogue. Although socially justified, Alexander's behind-the-scenes change from a disillusioned romantic to a bourgeois official cannot but affect his "artistic wholeness."[16]

Compared to Peter, however, his nephew is a "round" character, shown not only in his present action and in his natural setting, but with glimpses of childhood and school as well. Though Peter is said to have come from the same milieu, we know nothing of his past except that, in early youth, he picked yellow flowers from the lake for Alexander's aunt. In any case, his temperament is quite unaffected by his rustic past; indeed, he represents the exact opposite of everything that the country holds dear. This negative conception of Peter explains many of his artistic deficiencies, more, in any case, than are explained by Goncharov's own *ex post facto* arguments in *Better Late Than Never*. The reason why Alexander turned out "rounder and clearer," while the uncle is "paler," Goncharov writes, was that he embodied the old established life, while Peter represented something that was just coming into being (VIII, 74). While such a circumstance might cause a figure to be vaguely

conceived, Peter's papier-mâché quality stems rather from Goncharov's need for a sharp profile and his desire to maximize his
thematic thrust.

The abstract quality of Peter becomes manifest in several
ways. First, as the negation of provincial sentimentality he is
unceremonious to the point of incredible rudeness: he throws
Alexander's ring—a farewell gift from his country sweetheart—
out of the window, lights his cigar with Alexander's letter to
her, and treats his "collected works" like waste paper. His
brilliant performances, as excoriating critic, professional coun-
selor and apologist for his doctrine, are quite entertaining, but
at the cost of his human reality. Nor is he capable of change: a
"humorous" character with a bee in his bonnet about work and
rational living, he becomes quite absurd whenever he acts in
opposition to this built-in bias. His decision to turn over a
new leaf is a curious lapse of decorum on Goncharov's part,
certain effects, such as psychological depth, pathos, and basic
change being ruled out by Peter's very essence as a character.
Ultimately, anyway, all pretenses are dropped. Despite his embarrassment as Alexander keeps parroting his maxims in front
of Lizaveta in the final three-way scene, the old Peter is still
very much in evidence. His "reformed" variant is forgotten by
the author in order to sound a last mocking echo of some
favorite motifs, such as "yellow flowers," "sincere effusions,"
and "what's her name?"

However, many characters are almost wholly free of such
weaknesses, especially the women, whose portrayal was noted ·
with high praise by Belinsky and other critics. The only exception may be Julia Tafaev, a feminine exponent of romanticism.
A hysterical widow, she "gave herself up to her love the way
people give themselves up to opium and greedily drank the
heart's poison" (I, 205). This reckless abandon is less a personal
quality than an illustration of the effects of bad education. Prematurely aroused by unwise tutoring, Julia's emotions were
later artificially stimulated through novel reading. A travesty
of Pushkin's Tatyana in this respect, she is an old stereotype,
though effective enough as a female counterpart to Alexander.

Nadenka is another matter, eternally fresh in her girlish innocence and perverse charm. Goncharov's attempt, in retrospect,

to see her as the representative of a definite stage in the de-velopment of Russian womanhood seems heavy-handed. He writes in *Better Late Than Never:* "*I did not draw Nadenka, but the Russian girl of a certain circle, at a certain moment of that period.*" As compared to Pushkin's Olga and Tatyana, who married according to their parents' wishes, Nadenka—Goncharov says—breathes a slightly freer air and, in giving up Alexander for the Count, takes the first "*conscious step of the Russian girl*—tacit emancipation." However, she did not follow this up, he says, but "remained in ignorance" (VIII, 75). Though this representative quality may well be present, Nadenka is interest-ing chiefly because of her vivid reality, that of a girl awakening from the sleep of childhood.

Both Liza and Nadenka reveal the excellence of Goncharov's art when unhampered by didacticism or a program. Since they were necessary to the plot simply to put Alexander through his school of love, Goncharov's intuition had relatively free play in their creation. The portrayal of Liza, of course, is not very detailed, but memorable because of the skill with which the author has rendered the irresistible growth of passion in an inexperienced heart. She possesses a fervent nature under her placid exterior. Intrigued by Alexander's studied indifference, she is in the end overwhelmed by her own emotions. More playful than Liza, Nadya, too, is caught unawares by her feel-ings; but she knows intuitively how to handle them. There is a detached and whimsical air about her, one that is difficult to convey directly; consequently, we learn little from her formal portrait, done in an undistinguished manner, with the usual sprinkling of romantic clichés—eyes that emit a "penetrating ray," flash "like lightning" and "scorch," and an occasional hint of a "marble statue" in her appearance (I, 87).

It is in the dialogue and the use of gesture that the delight-fully capricious creature comes into her own. As against Alex-ander's hackneyed amorous folly, she is "cool," and with in-stinctive tact controls both her lover and her mother. The reader is offered no indiscreet glances into her mind, but her feelings are at her fingertips, whether she plays with a beetle, nips off ivy leaves or snatches away her hand (Ch. 4). And—a far more difficult accomplishment—in the course of a few brief scenes we see her change from a charming adolescent, a big child, to a mature young woman. The extent of her growth is shown by two incidents, in each of which her feelings can be inferred from her actions. In one, she pets a beetle and then, in sudden disgust, squashes it with her foot; in the other, the last glimpse we have of her, she is nervously playing the piano while Alexander demands to know his "fate." The fact that her feelings are conveyed indirectly, as objectified in her suddenly changing musical touch and her gestures, goes far to explain the perfect illusion here attained, both of a life-like scene and a living person.

Alexander's and Nadya's mothers form another pair, idolizing their offspring, both conform to the mother archetype. But while Mrs. Aduev is protective to the point of fussiness, her city counterpart is resigned to be dominated. And though both are comic figures, the source of their incongruities differs. Mrs. Aduev's world is defined by the narrow horizon of food, marriage and children, and her comic quality derives largely from her absolute horror at the godless practices in "foreign parts" like St. Petersburg. She is close to being a "humorous" character in the original sense of the term, her one thought being her son. The comedy of Mrs. Lyubetsky is partly one of situation, because of the inversion of the traditional mother-daughter relationship: Nadya had an "obedient mother" (I, 90). Clearly, Nadya does exactly what she wants, and the true state of things is symbolized by her mother's dozing in an armchair when Alexander comes visiting. A tendency to launch out into long monologues strengthens the impression of her remoteness from reality. Though the mold is the same as that used for Mrs. Aduev, the mother hen, the effect is sufficiently different to give her a distinctive stamp.

Goncharov's mastery is seldom as flawless as in his portraits of simple folk, caught with unfailing tact through a mannerism or a quirk of perspective. All his simple characters are slanted toward the physical and the idiosyncratic. Evsey, a twin to Avdey in "Ivan Savich Podzhabrin," remains skeptical of the "higher" life in the capital and at his return has praise only for the shoe polish, "good enough to eat" (I, 281). At the outset he is as sorry to leave his corner behind the stove as to part from Agrafena, his affectionate shrew of a sweetheart. Though prescribed by a time-honored tradition in the portraiture of plain folk, the earthiness of these figures may partly derive from their being drawn from life.[17] The same air of real-life profiles envelops Anton Ivanych, the "Wandering Jew," and Kostyakov, Alexander's petit-bourgeois friend; these look like two variants of the same comic type. Both live vicariously, Anton Ivanych in a crude parasitic way, Kostyakov like a sort of spiritual scavenger. While Anton Ivanych passes the time in ritual gluttony, Kostyakov thrives on human misfortune: he likes to be present at "extraordinary events like fights, fatal accidents, collapse of ceilings and so on, and with special enjoyment read reports on such accidents in the newspapers" (233). Both these figures have a definite folk flavor.

A clear dichotomy is evident in Goncharov's character portrayal in *A Common Story*. The central figures, those essential to his theme, are deficient in vividness, psychological verisimilitude, and depth. While partly due to literary constants such as the comic-ironic mode and a gently satiric intent, these deficiencies are aggravated by poor judgment and a tendency to strain for effect. After all, even a comic character must show a certain consistency in his behavior. These strictures apply even to Lizaveta, however sympathetic she may be; though present until the very end, she is far less vivid than Nadenka. But where he simply follows his talent for drawing without worrying what a figure means or represents, Goncharov is superb. Significantly, his successful characters—whether young girls on the verge of maturity, middle-aged mothers, hangers-on or servants—have one thing in common: they are all types who have been around, in life or in literature, for a long time, in the course of which they have developed an unmistakable aura, one which Goncharov knew how to capture.

VII *Structure and Texture in* A Common Story

In its composition, as in the portrayal of character, *A Common Story* combines a general tendency toward abstraction with sufficient nuances in structure and texture to avoid monotony. Its two balanced parts of six chapters each, with an epilogue, conform to the rules of classical symmetry. This neat shape, as well as the internal balance of two opposing figures which ultimately converge, has brought the charge of schematicism against the book. However, in its total result, affecting not only the novel's general design but also the interrelations of parts, whether situations, characters or scenes, the principle of symmetry produces formal intricacy. Over and above this, the novel's texture, with its wealth of verbal and other motifs, does much to diversify the overall scheme as well as Goncharov's scenic structure.

To show how symmetry may produce intricacy, we shall look briefly at the device of mirroring, a symmetrical relation that permeates the book. Affecting the treatment of both character and situation, this device usually functions ironically. Already we know that Alexander's second romance is an inverted reflection of his first and that, within the second romance, his image and double, Julia, more and more assumes the quality of a mocking mirror. But there are also less obvious mirrorings, possibly not consciously intended and evident only from a close reading of the text. For example, a connection is set up between Peter Aduev and the late Mr. Tafaev, a "man with all the attributes of a fiancé, that is, respectable rank, a good income and a star on his uniform—in short, career and fortune" (I, 204). Not only do we recognize in "career and fortune" Peter's chief slogan, but with Mr. Tafaev Peter also shares his knowledge of Russian "industrial needs" as well as his inability to recall his classical education. Moreover, Tafaev's marriage to Julia—she was eighteen, he forty-five—is a distorted reflection of Peter's to Lizaveta, just as Julia's hysteria is a more dramatic instance of Lizaveta's nervous ailment. Generally, the burlesque style in which Mr. Tafaev is presented, particularly his education (204–5), casts a dim light on Peter's culture and on his human worth.

Some of the most striking instances of "mirroring" are produced by the characters' habits, gestures, and other nuances of behavior. Highly interesting is the ironic parallel between the habits of Peter, especially as he grows older, and life in the provinces. Curiously, this champion of "active work" is almost constantly seen eating or dozing. While these activities are effective as means of deflating Alexander's windy sentimental talk, thematically they are chiefly associated with the stagnant life of the countryside. And so, subtly, here as in "The Evil Sickness" extremes meet.

All these crisscross patterns and reflexive references enliven the book, variegating its design with a web of half-submerged interrelations of parts and overlaying the obvious themes with a rich tapestry of meanings. Or, to change the figure, they set up little eddies of countermotion to the simple pressure of the theme, revealing its many possible twists and turns.

Goncharov's handling of scene demonstrates, on a smaller scale, the same combination of a simple structural scheme with a texture that at times is quite complex and poetic. The scheme is that of bathos, deliberate anticlimax, though the continual shifts from one mode to another might justify a term like modal counterpoint. The scenes are built on a tension of opposites, with some higher feeling or ideal set against material interests or physical need. The pathos of the leave-taking, for example, is undercut by a generous consumption of food; embarrassed by the maudlin talk of his mother, even Alexander mentions food. This sets a pattern for subsequent scenes in which the amorous ecstasies and torments of Alexander are deflated by his uncle, who warns him to close his "valve" (a reference to emotion as steam) and not to break things (Pt. I, ch. 3), emits satisfied grunts over a turkey dinner (Pt. I, ch. 6), and asks him to make out a bill for services rendered in the Surkov affair (Pt. II, ch. 3). Alexander's literary aspirations receive the same treatment: while reading the young man's poems, Peter yawns and fusses with his cigar, and as Alexander reads the rejection letter from the editor to him, he blows smoke rings (Pt. II, ch. 2). In scenes where Peter's sober, mocking voice is not heard, others take his place, such as Nadya's mother and Kostyakov. Alexander's most rapturous moment with Nadya is dispersed by Mrs. Lyubetsky's summons to buttermilk (Pt. II, ch. 4), and for the "pain" in his chest, anything but physical, she recommends opodeldoc (Pt. I, ch. 5). Kostyakov, like Peter, measures everything in terms of money, and during Alexander's misanthropic spell supplies a much needed complementary perspective.

Shifting perspectives also characterize the manner in which scenes are brought to a close. An excellent instance is Alexander's last departure from the Lyubetskys', which is turned into sheer farce. Characteristically, the farcical element is introduced by way of two lower-class characters, the janitor and his wife, whose crude but understandable suspicions bring Alexander's loudly expressed grief within an ordinary, down-to-earth context. One of the great masters of this technique is Shakespeare, as in the scene of "knocking at the gate" in *Macbeth*. Goncharov's success varies. In this case he may have slightly overdone the under-cutting: for example, the word "howl" (*revet*; used mostly about animals and children) is applied to Alexander's sobbing six times on less than half a page (I, 126), and the couple's specu-lations on what has happened have references to such "low" matters as theft, drunkenness, and hunger. The scene ends with a veritable monologue by the janitor about a possible loss of money. This is the end of Alexander's first romance.

By comparison, the way the affair with Julia is concluded (Pt. II, ch. 3) is more subtle, enriched with overtones by verbal and situational motifs. To appreciate this, however, it is neces-sary to refer back to the time of Alexander's first love, when he developed a habit of self-communion: "To converse with his own *self* was for him the highest pleasure. 'Only when alone with himself,' he wrote in some story, 'can man see himself, as in a mirror; only then does he learn to believe in human great-ness and dignity.'" As he is communing, Evsey enters, borne along by enthusiasm over his expertise in cleaning boots. "He considered this occupation his chief and almost only duty, and generally judged the value of a servant, or any other man, by his ability to clean boots" (I, 100). In a brief exchange, during which Alexander and Evsey accuse each other of being sense-lessly occupied, Evsey, using Peter's phrase, protests, "I do real work," and he "placed the boot on the table and looked lov-ingly at himself in the mirrorlike gloss of the leather" (101).

At the end of the affair with Julia, after his uncle, to Alexan-der's apparent regret, has managed to soothe the "betrayed" lady's feelings, this situation is repeated. When Peter leaves, having dropped some hints about the necessity of work, Evsey once more comes rushing in with his polished boot. The wax,

he says, is so good that the surface of the boot is "like a mirror"
(I, 222). This subtle little scene, the coda to a chapter-long
romance, speaks louder than any number of avuncular exhortations. The romantic mirror of self-communion is echoed in the
mirror of the boot, at once a ludicrous parody and a modest
symbol of being usefully occupied. The scene cuts the other
way, too, making light of the ponderous advice of the uncle.
Thus, through a kind of symbolism, along with the familiar
device of mirroring, the simple scenic structure is enriched
by a texture fraught with multiple meanings. Needless to say,
Alexander acts true to himself, showing his unregenerate egoism
by abusing Evsey and chasing him from the room.

VIII   *The Use of Motifs*

Motifs are such an important part of Goncharov's technique
in *A Common Story* that they deserve separate treatment. A
basic ingredient of dialogue, the verbal motif has far wider
ramifications. Indeed, the motif structure in *A Common Story*
is as essential as plot and theme, both of which acquire their
tonality and meaning from the way this structure is developed.
Thus, the contours of Alexander's story are fairly defined by
the image cluster associated with the Icarian-Christian theme
of flight and fall. Other important clusters are built around
words and images like "mirror," "cup," "crowd," "flowers," and
"money." Far from being self-sufficient units, these clusters tend
to interact and to form more and more complex units, at the
same time as they acquire new tones and meanings from different contexts.

This will become clear from examining a few of these motifs,
of which "mirror" has already appeared as a constituent of
scene. After the fiasco of his second romance, Alexander temporarily gives himself up to dissipation. "A flock of friends
appeared and, along with them, the inevitable *goblet* (*chasha*).
The friends contemplated their own faces in the foamy liquid
and then in their patent-leather boots" (I, 228). The word *chasha*
has previously figured in romantic contexts, in cliché metaphorical expressions like "cup of happiness" (100), "draining the cup
to the dregs" (179), and "cup of life" (199); now, in debased

form, it appears within the context of a drunken orgy, and no longer as a figure of speech but simply in the meaning of a drinking bowl. Both the reification of the figurative image and its debasement are an expression of a basic tendency of Goncharov's novel: to apprehend the reality beneath the layers of antiquated rhetoric. The ironic use of the mirror image, which here occurs in two permutations, continues the anti-romantic mockery of previous scenes.

It is worth noting that toward the end of the book "mirror" functions somewhat differently. First, Peter acts the bear in Krylov's fable "The Mirror and the Monkey," holding up a mirror to Alexander (I, 168–69), just as the latter has used Krylov to expose the weaknesses of his acquaintances. Secondly, one entire scene, Alexander's attendance at a concert with Lizaveta, acts as a *true* mirror to the young man. The successive moods of the musical offerings are described so as to suggest the stages of man's life, and Alexander sees his own life pass in review before him. "These sounds seemed, on purpose, to be relating with full intelligibility his past, his whole life, so bitter and disappointed" (253). Moreover, he sees himself in the German soloist and thereby recognizes his fault in having despised the "crowd": "I shunned the crowd, despised it, but that German, with his strong deep soul, his poetic nature, does not renounce the world and does not shun the crowd: he is proud of their applause. He understands that he is a barely noticeable link in the endless chain of humanity" (256). Thus the mirror motif, associated with things as varied in connotation as a pastoral lake with yellow flowers, polished boots, drinking bowls, and a concert, has a psychological amplitude ranging from romantic self-communion to its grotesque parody, with a somewhat bitter self-knowledge as the point of balance.

Two frequently recurring motifs related in tendency are "crowd" and "money"; the entire action of the novel may to a degree be understood as Alexander's reconciliation to these realities of life. Although in the first moment of rapture he speaks of being ready to "merge" with what he calls the "rationally active crowd" (I, 41) in the capital, up to the time of the concert he acts out the conventional romantic scorn for the masses and seeks solitude, or intimacy with a select few. The uncle's positive relationship to these masses, at least in theory, is evident from his holding up what he calls the "contemporary educated, thinking and acting" crowd as a model to his nephew (263). The money motif is deployed similarly, by a counterpoint method which constantly juxtaposes it to Alexander's nonmaterialistic values. Peter, the businessman, often talks about money and offers it to his nephew whenever he is in trouble. However, the latter keeps turning it down, refusing to give up his idealistic attitude. His ultimate adoption of Peter's values is appropriately reserved for the very last scene, where the uncle for the first time—and the last—allows his nephew to embrace him, while the latter takes money from him, also for the first and the last time: "This is an unusual [uncommon] occasion," says Alexander, punning as if he knows the novel's title.

A special kind of motif is formed by the use of literary allusion, particularly to the poetry of Pushkin. Such allusions are quite natural in a work focusing on an aspiring poet, and useful in recreating the intellectual climate of the period. However, Goncharov goes much further than this. One can truly speak of a complex Pushkin motif, associated with a multiplicity of opposing themes that ramify across the entire work.

Two poems, "The Poet and the Crowd" and "The Demon," provide most of the material for this motif. The first work consists of a dialogue between the "rabble" and the poet. The crowd motif already referred to is in Pushkin's poem associated with the most crass utilitarianism; the phrases "worm of the earth" and "son of the heavens" vividly formulate the opposed positions.[18] "We are born for inspiration/ For sweet sounds and for prayers," run the last two lines of the poem.[19] The poetic argument is closely reflected in a discussion between uncle and nephew about creativity. In one stanza Pushkin's poet says that, to the crowd, an earthenware pot is "more precious" than the Apollo Belvedere.[20] Without being impugned, the uncle's view is not so very different from that of the crowd. Interestingly, he owns a porcelain factory, and his concept of creativity seems to equate the gifts of an artisan who could improve the native porcelain with the "higher power" of a Shakespeare or a Dante (I, 56). Appropriately enough, after he has read Alexander's poetry he proposes they walk together to his factory (59).

"The Demon" is not only a source of verbal motifs, but offers a kind of archetypal pattern for the novel's action—one of disillusionment. In the poem, a demon visits the young persona, causing "the hours of delight and hope" to be overshadowed by a "sudden ennui." The soul of Pushkin's innocent youth, animated by the "sublime feelings" of freedom, fame, and love as well as by art, is filled with a "cold poison" through the "inscrutable glance" and the "caustic speeches" of his "evil genius," who dismisses beauty as a dream, flouts inspiration, and denies love and freedom.[21] Romantic as it may be, Alexander's identification of Peter with Pushkin's demon is a leitmotif in the book. Besides several direct references to demon,[22] there are subtle indirect allusions by way of imagery from the poem. First among these is the image of poison, in association with "glance" and "cold analysis," all connected with the uncle's "caustic speeches." "You poison . . . [life] with your glance," Alexander tells him (I, 69–70), and a little later he rejects his "cold analysis" on the ground that it would "poison" his happiness (83). This imagery is also used elsewhere, with implicit reference to the Pushkinian context. Warning Liza against reading Byron, another poet of disillusionment, Alexander enacts the role of an anti-demon as he compares the naïve and the analytical approach to life by way of an analogy. While one poet, he says, will show you the scent and beauty of a flower, another will show you only the "poisonous juice in its calyx . . . and then both beauty and fragrance will go lost for you." That he connects this side of the analogy with his uncle's "cold analysis" is clear from his advice to the young girl: "Do not seek poison, do not try to get at the origin of everything that goes on within and around us; do not seek unnecessary experience: it is not that which leads to happiness" (243).

IX *Literary Influences in* A Common Story

Whether the use of Pushkin just discussed comes under the heading of literary "influence" is a moot point. Altogether it is difficult to define precisely the relationship of Goncharov to Pushkin in *A Common Story*. On the one hand, the novel is saturated with allusions to Pushkin's work and, to a degree, young Aduev reenacts a Pushkinian role. On the other hand, the upshot of the work is as anti-Pushkin as it is anti-Romantic, for in A *Common Story* the only poet that Goncharov ever idolized (VIII, 263) provides thematic materials for an attitude and a *Weltanschauung* that he considered *passé*. Thus, while Pushkinesque in many of its themes, the novel at the same time represents a catharsis of the poet's influence; in fact, the free use of allusions shows that Goncharov was no longer under his sway. Since, then, he was perfectly aware of what he borrowed, other terms, whether take-off, parody, or thematic variations, might be more appropriate.

However, it is dubious whether the novel was *consciously* intended to reenact a variation of *Eugene Onegin*. Though quite candid about his general dependence on Pushkin's literary example, especially *Eugene Onegin* (1825–31), Goncharov never refers to the most obvious resemblance between his own novel and Pushkin's, namely, the parallel between the triangle Lensky-Olga-Onegin and that of Alexander-Nadya-Count Novinsky. While the only similarity between Onegin and Count Novinsky is their nobility, Olga and Nadya are essentially one and the same character, with allowance being made for Goncharov's more intensive treatment. As for Alexander, not only is he cut to the pattern of Lensky, as critics since Belinsky have been aware, but he seems set on enacting Lensky's role. When he suspects Nadya's interest in Novinsky, he recalls Lensky's thoughts about revenge on the day after the ill-fated ball (I, 114). Seeing the Count as a scheming seducer, Aduev, like Lensky, poses as the champion of innocence. When Nadya's "fickleness" is beyond doubt, Alexander wants to carry his allusive threat into action and fight the Count (132), a plan from which his uncle manages to dissuade him.

Some critics have seen Pushkin's suggestion of an alternate fate for Lensky as a model for Goncharov's treatment of the reconciled Aduev. Having first conjured up the image of a great future poet or sage, Pushkin says that maybe Lensky would have had an "ordinary" fate after all. And he paints a picture of comfortable middle age: the poetic ardor of youth has expired and he lives in the country, "happy and cuckolded," wearing a "quilted robe." Now he knows what life is about, eats and gets fat, and dies in the bosom of "his children, / Crying women and the doctors" (Ch. 6, st. 39).[23] During his visit to his mother's estate this fate seems a distinct possibility for Alexander, especially when he exchanges his "tight-fitting dress coat" for a "loose home-made robe" (I, 290). Perhaps to call to mind the "ordinary" lot envisioned for Lensky, Goncharov combines this transformation of Aduev with some echoes from a stanza in "Excerpts from Onegin's Travels," which Pushkin decided not to include in his work. Interestingly, the stanza in question contrasts the sublime images favored by the youthful Pushkin, such as desert, sea and mountains, with a number of homely images,[24] of which Goncharov, with slight inaccuracies, mentions *"the gray sky, the broken fence, the wicket gates, the muddy pond, the folk dance"* (290). Alexander, we are told, is beginning to "grasp the poetry" of these things. And yet, this was not to be his lot. One could argue, of course, that both the "ordinary" Lensky and Aduev end up as Philistines; however, the latter is adapted, at whatever cost, to the prose of a seemingly thriving life rather than to the "poetry" of a decaying order.

Among possible foreign influences two French novels, George Sand's *Horace* (1841) and Balzac's *Lost Illusions* (1837–39), have been prominently mentioned.[25] Goncharov may have been stimulated by these works to write a Russian counterpart to the European novel of disillusionment. One French critic has said that *Horace* and *A Common Story* fulfilled comparable tasks in their respective countries, namely, depicting a generation tragically deceived by the chimerical dreams of romanticism.[26] More specifically, Goncharov, who admired George Sand's subtle portrayal of character (VIII, 58), may have picked up a few hints from her profound exploration of the psychology of vanity and self-deception in *Horace*. *Lost Illusions,* a really great novel,[27] may have affected Goncharov more deeply. Though broader in scope than *A Common Story* and different in many of its themes, its basic outline is similar.

Lucien Chardon, alias de Rubempré, a young middle-class provincial of promise, is less a poet than a man with a poetic temperament. He is an indolent and weak-willed youth who, like Alexander Aduev, goes astray because of excessive imagination. After ruining his family by reckless living in Paris, where he has forged his brother-in-law's name on some bills, he returns home only to put them into deeper trouble still. Having caused his brother-in-law's arrest, he decides to end his life. However, before he manages to carry out his plan, he is picked up by a Spanish canon with aristocratic connections. This premature Nietzschean undertakes his reeducation. The canon, the epitome of cynical worldliness, is glad to find him so thoroughly disillusioned, making it possible for him to form the young man completely in his own image.

More striking than these general resemblances in the plot and the heroes are some detailed similarities in the imagery, despite its conventional quality. Considering Balzac's sparing use of figurative language, the abundance of imagery of flight in *Lost Illusions* is a coincidence worth noting. Not only does Lucien and his rustic friend David, later his brother-in-law, take soaring "flights" of fancy, but Lucien is frequently compared to royal birds, like eagles. And the imagery of falling is here, too. Both his mother and his sister, Eve, at one time or another think of him as "wallowing in the mire." There are also the yellow flowers, ostensibly a symbol of the poet. Finally, Peter's trademark, the cigar, is also the canon's.

While Goncharov may have wanted to accomplish something comparable to what Sand and, in particular, Balzac had done in their respective novels, his talent was very different and something new emerged. Aduev's experience is truly a sentimental education or even purgation, in the course of which he becomes transformed into a new person, whereas Horace retains his self-deceptions to the very end. Chardon does not, and here is a close link between him and Alexander Aduev. However, Balzac paints a broad canvas on which social, political, and economic processes are minutely analyzed, along with manners and the characters' psychology; Goncharov's focus is narrow, largely concentrated on the experiences of one person. Yet, in his character portrayal he is no match for Balzac, though his artistry in some ways is finer, as a study of his imagery and motif structure demonstrates. Despite Goncharov's possible indebtedness to these novels, *A Common Story* is a wholly original work; any elements that may have been borrowed are completely assimilated.

CHAPTER 4

Oblomov

THE publication of *Oblomov* was a landmark in Russian literature. Initially overshadowed by Turgenev's *A Nest of the Gentry,* it was catapulted to fame by Dobrolyubov's article "What Is Oblomovism?" which came out in May, 1859. Prince Kropotkin reports that the appearance of *Oblomov* was a far greater event than the publication of a new work by Turgenev.[1] Its characters assumed a life of their own, especially Oblomov; they evoked a sense of recognition in the reader and were discussed as real, living people.

The exceptionally long period of gestation may partly account for the book's profound appeal. At its publication in *Notes of the Fatherland* in 1859, ten years had passed since the appearance of the fragment "Oblomov's Dream" and twelve years since the novel's conception. Apart from ordinary official duties, which always claimed the better part of his time, for nearly three years Goncharov was a world traveller. After his return from Japan in 1855, he spent a couple of years editing his travel sketches, based upon the log book, assorted letters to friends, and the journal he kept during the voyage. *The Frigate "Pallada,"* which makes up two volumes of his collected works, came out in book form in 1858. In the meantime, during an exceptionally prolific summer the year before in Marienbad, Goncharov all but completed *Oblomov;* what remained to do was mostly revision.

With such a record of activity, Goncharov was clearly no "Oblomov," a byword for a sluggard, and conversely Oblomov is not a direct image of his creator. On the other hand, we know that already in his twenties Goncharov used to flaunt his indolence and was in the habit of signing himself "Prince de *Len'* " (meaning "laziness"), a take-off on Prince de Ligne. There is unquestionably a close connection between Goncharov's biography and his fiction, but it is not simply one of self-dramatization. In *Better Late Than Never* he says he could only write about what he had himself experienced (VIII, 113), but he always insists on the shaping and transforming power of the imagination. Even his reminiscences temper *Wahrheit* with *Dichtung*, this being for him the only possible way of achieving artistic truth (VII, 225). In his fiction an important element of *Dichtung* derives from imaginary extensions of his own major predilections, such as the indolence intrinsic to an "artistic contemplative nature"[2] and its opposite, bustling activity. Through his heroes he gives hyperbolized expression to his own innate possibilities, while embodying them in forms which, in Hamlet's phrase, showed the "body of the time his form and pressure." Thus, thirty-two or thirty-three year old Ilya Oblomov, a provincial landowner living in St. Petersburg, is a type of his class—the middle or petty gentry—at a difficult period for the Russian landowner; but at the same time Goncharov projects through Oblomov an imaginative extension of himself.

The story of *Oblomov* is extremely simple. In a novel that is thematically poised on inaction, the lack of a complex plot is quite appropriate. The first of the four parts, following an "all life in a day" scheme, shows Oblomov comically unable to get out of bed. He receives some visitors and has an epic dream of his childhood home, Oblomovka. With the beginning of Part II, using the half-German businessman Stolz as his prod, the author puts his major character through his paces. Stolz introduces him to Olga Ilinsky (the complication), and Oblomov undergoes an agonizing love affair with the charming young girl, who is set on curing him of his apathy. A critical moment arrives when—in panic—he sends Olga a parting letter, though the seriousness of his intention is mocked by his subsequent spying on her as she reads it. The result of this pathetic-humorous interlude is that, at the end of Part II, Oblomov falls down "at the feet" of his bride-to-be (the climax). However, soon he retreats, in a critic's words, with all the "faultless strategic skill of the neurotic."[3] His hesitations, fears, and unconscious deceptions during the next few months compel Olga to realize that she has made a mistake; as she tells him, she has been in love with an imaginary figure (IV, 382). Convinced that he is incorrigible, she drops him, deeply grieved by the futility of her mission (the dénouement). This affair extends roughly through Parts II and III.

Meanwhile, since Oblomov's move to suburban Vyborg, a contrary force has been at work, namely, the elemental attraction of his landlady, Agafya Matveyevna Pshenitsyn, a widow who in Part IV first becomes his mistress and then his wife (the aftermath). Juxtaposed with Oblomov's decline into the petit-bourgeois routine of Vyborg, we observe Stolz moving in to replace his friend in the affections of Olga. In an epilogue we are informed of Oblomov's end; eight or nine years after the time of the opening chapter he dies of a stroke—appropriately, in his sleep. His son, Andrey, named for Stolz, is given over to his successful namesake for upbringing, so as to enable him to take over the family estate which Stolz has looked after in the meantime. In the last scene we meet Zakhar, Oblomov's valet, begging in the streets of St. Petersburg; though fallen on evil days, he refuses to leave the city where his master is buried. The four parts of the book could be called Sleep, Awakening, Relapse and Sleep, respectively.

Stolz from beginning to end endeavors to arouse Oblomov, while a pair of crooks, Tarantiev and Agafya's brother, Mukhoyarov, constitute an evil opposing force. A sworn enemy of Stolz, as of all men of "foreign" background, big, hulky, furiously active Tarantiev is Oblomov's chief parasite.[4] Oblomov's inability to live without parasites is inherited from Oblomovka, where such people were a necessary adjunct of life. Both Tarantiev and another parasite, the faceless Alexeyev, serve as distorting mirrors to their host. Tarantiev, besides, plays a fateful role in his life. Frustrated professionally, he allows the "theory of graft and fraud" (IV, 42) instilled in him by his father to invade and dominate his personal relations. It is this crook that the naïve and unpractical Oblomov, with his fatalistic trust in words like "perhaps, maybe, and somehow" (99), chooses to consult about his "two misfortunes," namely, his landlord's request to vacate the apartment and an upsetting letter from the steward of his estate. In collusion with Mukhoyarov, Tarantiev writes an outrageous lease, which Oblomov signs unread. Though he has no desire to move to Vyborg, his hands are now tied: he has no money, and court action is threatened if he breaks the lease. This intrigue à la Dickens gathers increasing momentum when, to avoid going to the country himself, Oblomov seeks the advice of crafty Mukhoyarov, who finds an agent for him among his friends. Together, the three of them mercilessly fleece their gullible victim, who is rescued only through the arrival of Stolz.

When their designs are thwarted by Stolz's leasing of Oblomovka, Tarantiev and Mukhoyarov resort to outright blackmail. Exploiting Oblomov's growing interest in his sister, Mukhoyarov threatens him with serious consequences unless he signs an IOU for 10,000 rubles to his sister, who in turn is forced to issue an identical paper to her brother. Thus, both Oblomov and his landlady are ruined, until Stolz again intervenes to expose the nefarious scheme, enabling Oblomov to enjoy a period of tranquillity before he dies.

This brief summary gives only the vaguest idea of Goncharov's masterpiece. The outer format is obviously biographical, as in so many contemporary French and English novels; together with the prehistory, the action extends over several decades of the hero's life. Because of the pitiless deterioration of a potentially noble figure, the book has been called a psychological tragedy, while Georg Lukács uses the term "novel of disillusionment."[5] But *Oblomov* also has much in common with the novel of everyday life (*bytovoi roman*), since it contains a microscopic treatment of the routine of life, its sea of trivia. The critic Druzhinin saw it in epic terms as encompassing the "entire live of a given sphere, a given epoch, and a given society."[6] Moreover, it also fulfils a key requirement of the chronicle novel; for despite the paucity of allusion to contemporary events, the book creates a strong sense of the ground swell of time, mostly because of the changes at Oblomovka. These varied contents suggest that we have to do with a work *sui generis*. The same is true for the central character, who like Hamlet or Faust invites any number of different interpretations.

Partly because of its great complexity, partly to convey a sense of its finely woven texture, the following examination of the novel will begin with some fairly close reading, combined with analysis of structure. It seems wiser initially to ask how the parts of this intricate organism interact than what it all means.

I   A *Picaresque Duo: Oblomov and Zakhar*

A notable feature of *Oblomov* is the enormously long exposition, occupying more than one entire part and accounting for nearly one third of the novel's length. Most of this material deals with the central character, whose personality, unlike that of young Aduev, is given at the outset. Moreover, in the exceptionally long chapter "Oblomov's Dream" the author projects a total image of the socio-psychological matrix from which this personality developed.

Oblomov is first seen in the horizontal, his "normal state," clad in a dressing gown, a "genuine Oriental robe without the slightest suggestion of Europe." Man and garment are one: the robe is "soft and supple, his body did not feel it; it obeyed the slightest movement of his body, like a docile slave" (IV, 8). Along with his slippers, his bed and robe will accompany Oblomov as leitmotifs throughout most of the story.

In describing Oblomov's room, Goncharov follows Gogol, but transcends his technique. In *Dead Souls* the surroundings express the man; everything on Sobakevich's estate is big and sturdy, while on Plyushkin's things decay and rot from the sheer force of miserly cumulation. The minute details in the description of Oblomov's apartment—the "dusty cobwebs" around the pictures, the dirty plate with remnants of last night's supper, the crumb-covered table; the old newspaper, the open pages of the book, yellow and with a coating of dust; the "startled fly" emerging from the inkwell at the dip of the pen (IV, 9–10) —all these minutiae of Oblomov's immediate surroundings reveal the pupil of Gogol. However, the indifference manifested by this condition of "neglect and untidiness" has a quality of sublimity about it that prevents it from being simply a negative thing. Anyone who can look at the furniture of his study "coldly and absently, as though wondering who had brought . . . all that stuff there" (9), must live elsewhere, in a different dimension. Cut off from the actual and finding "happiness" only through dream and through his "plan" for improving his estate, Oblomov sees life as "divided into two parts: one consisted of work and boredom—these words were synonymous to him— the other of rest and peaceful joy" (58).[7] Clearly, such a character defies portrayal by sheer accumulation of everyday details; he can only be adequately presented in terms of his inner world. But, for the sake of convenience, we shall postpone the discussion of "Oblomov's Dream" and follow the order of the narrative.

Most of the action in Part I is verbal, consisting of the surly exchanges between Oblomov and Zakhar and of Oblomov's discussions with a string of visitors, who want him to join their celebration of May Day. The relationship between Oblomov and Zakhar calls to mind Don Quixote and Sancho Panza. Both Oblomov and Quixote are dreamers and their servants are down-to-earth men. But here the similarities end. What is more, Oblomov could be seen as an anti-Quixote. Far from setting out to kill dragons and fight windmills, Oblomov has contempt for action and prefers to stay in bed: he likes his "visions" pure. Secondly, Zakhar is so closely associated with his master that he lives in a sort of symbiosis with him. He is essentially a grotesque counterpart to Oblomov on a lower social level. Finally, whatever picaresque movement this part of the story may have, is in reverse. The use of a succession of callers is reminiscent of a morality play like *Everyman,* in which the title character is visited by a number of allegorical figures.

Oblomov's three first visitors have symbolic names that show up the conventional roles they play. Volkov—derived from *volk,* "wolf"—wants to be a lion but is merely an infatuated dandy on a social whirligig. Sudbinsky's fate (*sud'ba*) is to be overworked as a successful official about to make a "good match." Finally, Penkin, with a name suggesting sheer froth (*pena*) and the nuisance of "skin" on milk (*penka*), is a fashionable journalist excited about the latest exposé of social corruption. Oblomov parries these tempters, sleazy near-burlesque types of no psychological depth, with shivers, yawns, frowns, and shakes of the head. They have no relation whatever to his life.

It is different with Zakhar, his permanent companion, who is anything but a servant stereotype. His ambivalent feelings toward his master, alternately abused and idolized, show his psychological complexity. Technically, his chief importance consists in being a symbol of Oblomov's past, for Zakhar has adapted even less to city ways than Oblomov. An elderly man now, he still acts and dresses as in his early days at Oblomovka. At a time when the old patriarchal order is changing, the servants alone preserve the tradition. As Goncharov writes: "Only the gray-haired servants of the family preserved and handed down to one another faithful memories of the past, prizing them as something holy" (IV, 12). Therefore, though "torn under the arm and showing his shirt," his gray coat is treasured by Zakhar as a "dim reflection of bygone greatness" (11). Ironically, even Oblomov's whims seem to evoke the great past, for without them "he somehow would not have felt he had a master over him; without them there would have been nothing to bring back his youth, the country they had left years ago, and the legends of the old house . . ." (11–12). Goncharov suggests that even his whiskers, big enough for birds to nest in, may be dear to him precisely "because in childhood he had seen many old servants with that old-fashioned aristocratic adornment" (12).

And yet, even Zakhar is tainted with newfangledness. Belonging to two "different epochs," he has inherited from one a "boundless devotion to the Oblomov family, from the other, the later one, subtlety and corrupted morals" (IV, 70). In a tour de force of comic portraiture (Pt. I, ch. 7) the author creates a vivid and entertaining semblance of a real person, at the same time projecting a series of ironical contrasts which highlight the theme of social change. While the old servants were models of sobriety, Zakhar drinks with his friends "at the master's expense"; whereas they were "chaste as eunuchs," he visits "a lady of doubtful virtue"; while the old-time servants "guarded their master's money better than any coffer," Zakhar is addicted to petty thievery (70–71). But despite these signs of being in tune with the times, Zakhar still belongs to the old order. Indirectly, his portrayal shows how out of place Oblomov is in the cold, impersonal, socially buzzing atmosphere of the capital. In his crude, clumsy and, above all, lazy rustic ways, Zakhar is an anachronism in the city, and his master is a spiritual exile.

II *"Oblomov's Dream"*

The spiritual home of both is Oblomovka. This is no "nest of the gentry," a synonym for culture, enlightenment and a refined humanity. Rather, it is an old-fashioned estate located in a

backwater close to the borders of Asia. A masterpiece of evoca-
tive description, interspersed with brief dialogues and typical
incidents, Goncharov's chapter on Oblomovka (Pt. I, ch. 9)
creates an entire world, from its placid landscape and unhurried
life to its customs and beliefs. The form is a literary "dream,"
which is by no means a real psychological experience. True, the
author suggests that Oblomov is actually reliving his past, as
when, seeing his mother, the dreamer "even in his sleep . . .
thrilled with joy and ardent love for her; two warm tears slowly
emerged from under the sleeper's eyelashes and rested on his
cheeks" (IV, 110). Nevertheless, the value of the "dream" as
pure experience, an act of unconscious memory taking Oblomov
back to his childhood home, is questionable. In particular,
neither Oblomov the dreamer nor Ilyusha, the dreamer as a
child, can possibly appreciate the author's irony. And the associations are poetically rather than psychologically motivated, as
the author composes a sort of literary symphony or a tone poem
of the past. Apart from its intrinsic value, its chief function is
to explain the personality of Oblomov.

As the narrative proceeds, it becomes clear that the ethos of
patriarchal life is at the root of Oblomov's malaise. However, as
in any neurotic condition, this knowledge is not accessible to
the subject. The desire of Oblomov, uttered as he enters his
enchanted world, to know why he is as he is, is not answered:
"'It must be . . . it's because . . .' He made an effort to form
the words but could not" (IV, 102). It is the reader who discovers the answer, as this highly structured pre-Freudian dream
unfolds before him, adding another dimension to Oblomov's
character.

Chronologically, the dream deals mainly with two periods of
Ilya's life; first, he is a child of seven, then a boy of thirteen
or fourteen. The several parts, devoted to such facets of life as
the daily routine, holidays, folklore, and attitudes to the outside
world, are all unified by tone and imagery, and by periodic
returns to the dreamer. The author contemplates the scene with
Olympian calm; the occasional bursts of lyricism are balanced
by flashes of irony. The imagery has a pastoral quality, heightened by Biblical and classical allusions. The eternal recurrence
of Oblomovka life emerges through a series of neatly-placed

sound motifs. All in all, the dreamer's world is vividly real, dense with sensory content, while the whole is veiled in an aura of myth.

The landscape of this "blessed" spot suggests an earthly paradise exempt from the ills of mortality. It has "no sea, no high mountains, cliffs or precipices and no dense forests—nothing grand, gloomy, or wild" (IV, 102).[8] Nature at Oblomovka is domesticated; the sky is not a remote and indifferent blue, but "stretched low overhead like a trusty parental roof, as if to preserve the chosen spot from every misfortune" (103). Personifying nature, Goncharov underscores its oneness with the human world: the sun towards autumn seems reluctant to withdraw, the river runs "merrily, sporting and playing" (104), and the summer rain splashes down "like the big hot tears of a person overcome with sudden joy" (105). But if nature is close to man, man in turn is close to nature, unperturbed by thought. Barely awakened, consciousness easily lapses into sleep: the gentle murmur of the river "lulls one sweetly into drowsiness" and death itself "comes unnoticed like sleep" (104). The leitmotif of sleep, increasing in amplitude as the dream continues, is thus subtly introduced already in the description of the landscape. Life in the village, too, is "still and sleepy": "only the flies swarm and buzz in the sultry air" (107).

In describing a typical day at Oblomovka as seen by little Ilya, Goncharov has his eye on the psychology of growth. From the very outset an evident conflict exists between the lively natural impulses of the boy and the well-regulated life around him. When his mother takes him to the icon to pray in the morning, he repeats the prayer after her "absentmindedly, looking out of the window through which the morning freshness and the scent of lilacs poured into the room" (IV, 111). In Part II the lilac, called "the flower of life," will be the chief motif of Oblomov's romance with Olga, and together with a bit of wormwood it will bloom on Oblomov's grave. What the lilac stands for is unattainable because Ilya lives in a kind of hothouse, unnaturally overprotected; his fussy nurse frustrates his attempts to explore the world around him and, finding no outlet, his energies "drooped and withered" (146). Forced into the role of a pure observer, he takes in the decaying house, the drowsy garden, the general ambience of idleness; and he watches the solemn rituals of preparing food, the heroic postprandial siesta, the Homeric thirst quenched in oceans of tea and kvass. The siesta suggests a canvas by Breughel: the whole household lies prostrate, noisily asleep "wherever the heat or the heavy dinner had overcome them." But the genre quality is heightened by a pervasive image: "It was an all-engulfing, irresistible sleep, a veritable semblance of death," the author comments, with a possible allusion to the fairy tale *The Sleeping Beauty.* Occasionally, someone would wake up from thirst, take a quick drink and then "fall back on the bed as if shot" (116). And all the time Ilya's "sensitive mind, impregnated by the examples before him, was unconsciously tracing a plan for his life in accordance with the life around him" (113).

The fairy-tale section which follows shows an important part of Oblomovka culture and education; in fact, fairy tales seem to be the chief spiritual sustenance of children at Oblomovka. Part of this sequence forms a sort of mini-Oblomovka, one of pure fancy, within the fictively real one. Oblomov dreams how his nurse told him "of an unknown country where there was no night or cold and where miracles were happening all the time: rivers flowed with milk and honey, no one ever worked, and fine fellows like Ilya Ilyich, and maidens more beautiful than words can tell, did nothing but make merry all day long" (IV, 120). A good fairy chooses for her favorite "some quiet, harmless man—in other words some sluggard," who has nothing to do but eat and who marries some "peerless beauty," Militrisa Kirbitievna. Then Goncharov goes on to make a didactic point: because these tales avoided reality, he says, "the mind and the imagination, imbued with make-believe, remained enslaved by it till old age." For though Ilya eventually saw through the pretense and even made fun of this fairy-tale world, "his smile was not sincere and was accompanied by a secret sigh: the fairy tale had become confused with life in his mind and at times he was sad that the fairy tale was not life and life not a fairy tale" (121). The effect of the horror stories he heard was no less harmful, the author suggests. They peopled the boy's imagination with "strange phantoms" (123), and even after he no longer believed in phantoms "there remained a residue of fear and unaccountable anguish." At the sight of a corpse or when alone in a room, he would still feel "a tremor of that ill-boding anguish implanted in his soul as a child" (124).

A sort of epic of the "unexamined life," according to Socrates not worth living,[9] "Oblomov's Dream" shows life as a closed cycle, every day alike and each year repeating its predecessor. Typical, or habitual, narrative is the natural vehicle for a routine of this kind and Goncharov uses it successfully, first in presenting an ordinary day at Oblomovka and later in evoking a "long winter evening." The conversation about visitors, births, deaths, and omens on this latter occasion is pointedly inane. The atmosphere is conveyed concretely by means of a series of auditory motifs. "All was still; only the tread of Ilya Ivanovich's heavy home-made boots, the muffled ticking of a clock in its case on the wall, and the occasional snapping of a thread . . . disturbed the profound stillness" (IV, 132). Variations are provided by communal yawning and fits of laughter. Apropos of next to nothing, their mirth rolls in resounding peals throughout the house as they laugh in unison "like the Olympian gods" (135). This laughter is like a force of nature rushing in to fill the inner vacuum of their lives. When it subsides, the more subdued sound motifs are recapitulated: "As before the only sounds were the ticking of the clock, the tread of Oblomov's boots and the light snapping of . . . thread" (135). More than just a fact of life, to them this monotony is an ideal: "They would have been utterly miserable if tomorrow were not like today and if the day after tomorrow were not like tomorrow" (137). When, in a rare moment, the father senses the intrusion of change in their lives, he reflects: "How much better it would be if every day were like the day before and tomorrow just like yesterday!" (134).

The Oblomovs do, of course, have a means of neutralizing change, namely ritualism. All events, from the momentous triad of birth, marriage, and death to the most trivial such as visits and dinner parties, are strictly managed in accordance with tradition. Living by the Church calendar, "they reckoned the time by holy days, by the seasons of the year, by various family and domestic occurrences, and never referred to dates or months" (IV, 133). Thus, time at Oblomovka is a highly regulated pattern, an archetype reminiscent of the "eternal return" intrinsic to archaic ontology. According to the anthropologist Mircea Eliade, the purpose of ritual in what he calls "premodern societies" was to recreate the cosmogonic act *in illo tempore*, to effect a merging of the present with the time of the beginning and thus annul history and change.[10] With Christianity functioning as myth, the dichotomy of mythic and profane—that is, meaningless—time made by Eliade has a clear counterpart in Oblomovka existence: "Their hearts throbbing with excitement, they waited for some ceremony, feast or rite, and then, having christened, married or buried a man, they forgot all about him and sank back into their usual apathy, from which some similar occasion—a name day, a wedding, etc.—roused them once again" (127).

The antihistorical bias of primitive man, expressing itself in a need "periodically to abolish" history,[11] is clearly present, though in attenuated form, in Oblomovka. It is demonstrated not only by the incident of the letter, an unwelcome intrusion from the larger world, but also by the handling of Ilya's education. The arrival of the letter is an unprecedented event; failing to fit into the traditional pattern, it represents a threat. After they survive opening it, answering the sender's request for a beer recipe is postponed to fit in with the holy-day pattern, and eventually the whole thing seems to be forgotten. Anyway, "it is not known whether or not Filip Matveyevich ever received the recipe" (IV, 141). History, in a manner of speaking, was cheated. Similarly, the need for education, though recognized in a crude utilitarian way, is successfully bypassed. Their life being self-contained, "they had no need of anything; life flowed by them like a quiet river, and all they had to do was to sit upon the bank of that river and watch the inevitable events which presented themselves . . ." (126–27). Moreover, "their way of life was ready-formed and was taught to them by their parents, who in turn had received it ready-made from the grandparents," and so on *ad infinitum*. With traditional wisdom giving all the answers, they "never troubled about any obscure moral or intellectual problems"; in no hurry to explain "the meaning of life" to a child, they viewed books merely as a source of problems that "gnaw at your heart and mind and shorten life." In

conjunction with their concept of work as a "punishment im-
posed upon our forefathers" (126), these attitudes indicate the
great odds against a child at Oblomovka receiving an effective
education and entering the stream of history.

Appropriately, the "dream" ends with a picture of Ilya, at the
age of thirteen or fourteen still caught between his natural desire
for healthy activity and the Oblomovka way of life, now about
to become second nature to him. We watch the holiday celebrations—the traditional culture—interfere with his school term
at old Stolz's and see his character become tainted by a parasitic existence in which his every whim is carried out by a horde
of lackeys. At this point, Goncharov hints, it may already have
been too late to start educating Ilya, whose "heart and mind"
had been imbued with the slow lazy rhythms of Oblomovka
from the cradle. "Who can tell how early the seed of intellect
begins to develop in a child's brain?" he asks, suggesting that
even before he can walk or talk a baby may perceive what goes
on around it. Perhaps Ilyusha's "childish mind had decided long
ago that the only way to live was the way the grown-ups around
him lived. How, indeed, could he have decided otherwise?" (IV,
125). Yet, the final vignette raises the nostalgic possibility of a
different fate as Ilya rushes out of the house one winter day to
join the neighboring children in a snowball fight. The whole
household is mobilized to retrieve the missing boy, who is kept
"three days in bed, though only one thing could have done him
any good—playing snowballs again" (147).

III *Story and Structure in* Oblomov

The rest of the novel seems like a demonstration of the impossibility of another fate for Oblomov. The signs of real conflict which appear in him as soon as Stolz assumes his role as
prompter, are presented in mock-heroic fashion, a mode which
does not permit basic change. By way of an ironic parallel with
Hamlet, the author shows Oblomov trying to make up his mind:

What was he to do now? Go forward or remain where he was? This
Oblomov question was for him deeper than Hamlet's. To go forward
meant suddenly to throw his loose robe not only off his shoulders but

also from his mind and soul, to sweep the cobwebs from his eyes along
with the dust and cobwebs on the walls and recover his sight again!

The outcome may be predicted from his attempt to rise: " 'Now
or never!' 'To be or not to be!' Oblomov raised himself a little
from the chair, but when his feet did not find his slippers at
once he sat down again" (IV, 193).

The principal stages of the action are marked by variations
on such motifs, significant details which assume new meanings
as they occur in different contexts. It is as if the action proceeds
on two tracks or levels, that of event and motif. The robe functions as an effective vehicle of both story and theme; with an
amazing economy of means Goncharov conveys the vicissitudes
of its owner's psychological condition through his behavior
toward it. At the height of his love for Olga, Oblomov does not
wear the robe; except for a single lapse (IV, 235), he even stays
away from his inviting sofa. With his move to the Vyborg district, however, the situation changes. Though we are told that
his robe has been put away in a closet, he "sometimes casually
lay down on the sofa to read a book," a good intention under-
mined by its context. Moreover, various Oblomovka motifs, such
as the "deep clucking of the broody hen, the peeping of the
chicks and the twitter of the canaries and siskins" (323), show
the underlying drift of Oblomov's life. From now on, these and
other sound motifs recur regularly. The gradualness of his relapse is conveyed by the return of more and more of the old
familiar objects. Once, Oblomov lies "carelessly on the sofa
playing with his slipper: he dropped it on the floor, threw it in
the air, twirled it, and picked it up from the floor with his foot
when it fell" (328). He is subconsciously flirting with his
old life. By the middle of Part III he already sleeps after dinner.
And now, in good time, Agafya brings his old robe out of the
storeroom for washing and mending. Praising the "nice material,"
she says it will still last him a long time (347). After returning
from his final visit to Olga at the very end of Part III, he "hardly
noticed" Zakhar's slipping the refurbished garment across his
shoulders. Oblomov's life has come full circle. All that can
happen from now on, to the robe as to Oblomov's life, is that
they fall apart.

Many kinds of conflict are implicit in the motifs used: between country and city, tradition and modernism, childhood and adult responsibility, stagnation and striving, passionate love and mere sensual indulgence. All of these oppositions are rooted in a polarity within time itself, between continuity and change. Oblomov is unable to come to grips with time, finding transience, mutability—always a part of the human experience of time—too painful to bear. Therefore, relinquishing "all his youthful hopes . . . and all the bright, bittersweet memories that make the heart beat faster" (IV, 63), he tries to reduce time to a dimensionless point. Taking refuge from the real within his "poetic moment" out of time—as when he prefers daydreaming of Olga to actually being with her—Oblomov may escape suffering, but at the cost of near petrifaction. Even so, his escape is not complete: occasionally the "forgotten memories" and "unfulfilled dreams" return to consciousness to disturb his quasi-hermetic state, causing great anguish of soul before he can once more resume his reverie (487).

In conveying the flux of life and the characters' attitudes toward it, Goncharov uses organic imagery. The love of Olga and Oblomov grows like a flower, which reaches its time of blossoming and then withers; a spray of lilac accompanies their romance throughout. Where the actual flower is not present, its image is evoked by association of place (IV, 238) or, more subtly, by a lilac motif in the design of Olga's embroidery (241); there are also several mentions of "lilac" dresses. Oblomov receives the lilac, "the flower of life," from Olga after complaining that "the flower of life has fallen, only the thorns remain" (242). Through this metaphor of transience Oblomov expresses his pessimistic sense of life, while Olga uses similar expressions affirmatively; on her lips a word like "wither" expresses a positive acceptance of time and its changes. Thus, when Oblomov alludes to her "stern 'never'" spoken in a moment of anger (272), she softly answers, "It will wither." To him, on the other hand, the idea of withering seems menacing, as he realizes that even the most rapturous moments "will pass, like the lilac." Recalling his dream of love, he reflects:

"I thought it would hang over lovers like a hot noon and that nothing would stir or breathe in its atmosphere. But even in love there is no rest; it too is always moving somewhere, on and on . . . 'like all life,' Stolz says. And the Joshua who could tell it, 'Stand still and do not move!' has not yet been born." (273)

In this way, the lilac not only registers the changing course of their romance, but also dramatizes Oblomov's and Olga's psychology and values through their attitudes to time.

The further use of the lilac motif seems to universalize the problem faced by Oblomov. For when Olga breaks with him she hopelessly applies the image of withering to her own past (IV, 381), and afterwards she falls into an Oblomovesque apathy. During Stolz's courtship she thinks in terms of Oblomov's fatalistic language: the "flower of life has faded forever" (419), the "flower of life had fallen" (422). Just as Olga tried her best to reconcile Oblomov to transience, so Stolz frees Olga from her temporary fixation on the past and brings her back into the stream of life. When she raises the question of her past, Stolz tells her, "It will wither like your lilac" (434), after which he exhorts her to begin life afresh with him. In a last variation the motif of "withering" occurs in the final chapter dealing with Olga and Stolz. Like all else, their relationship has changed: "There were no sounds of kisses and laughter, no tremulously musing conversations in the grove, among the flowers, at the festival of life and nature. All that had 'withered and gone'." But not everything passes away: for an "unfading and indestructible love, strong as the life force, could be seen in their faces. . ." (476).

The "language of flowers" is only the most striking aspect of the intricate artistry of *Oblomov*, a novel notable for an unusually close interaction between the various elements of composition. Just as Oblomov's manner of dress and furniture, along with the externals of life at Oblomovka, transcend realism and become symbols of a way of life, so nature during the romance of Olga and Oblomov intimately merges with their lives. Compositionally, this means that setting and character, event and image, nature and psychology become so closely interwoven that a texture results to which the word "poetic" is appropriate.

Though nothing unusual, the parallel between the love affair and the seasonal cycle gives rise to a rich poetic imagery. Gon-

charov seems to orchestrate the "living concord" Olga perceives
between herself and things in nature (IV, 244). When summer
was at its height, "ardent summer reigned within them too, with
occasional clouds gathering and disappearing." If Oblomov is
troubled, a bright look from her sets everything right again:
"once more feeling flowed smoothly like a river, reflecting the
changing patterns of the sky" (275). Conversely, Olga's lapse
into "a kind of somnambulism of love," seemingly a euphemism
for sexual passion, takes place on a "hot and sultry" evening
under a "heavily overcast" sky (277). It is dark and suffocating,
and Olga's breath on his cheek is as hot as the evening. But
"despite the frequent alterations in the rosy atmosphere" (282),
in Part II the horizon is mostly clear: their tribulations pass as
quickly as clouds in a summer sky.

However, when they return to the city, the natural setting for
their love is missing: "the blooming summer poem of their love
seemed to have come to an end, proceeded more lazily as if
short of substance" (IV, 311). And by the time they have a rendezvous in the Summer Garden, a city park, the grounds are
covered with fallen leaves (Pt. III, ch. 5). At the breakup,
Olga says farewell to bright images of summer: "The summer
. . . the park . . . do you remember? I am sorry for our avenue, the lilac . . . It has all grown into my heart: it hurts to
tear it out!" (381). Another season imbues her soul, the tears
streaming "coldly and cheerlessly, like autumn rain pitilessly
drenching the fields" (381). As Oblomov afterwards sits in his
chair, the long discarded robe around his shoulders and his
heart "dead," the surroundings are "plunged in sleep and darkness." Next morning when, numb and feverish, he walks over
to the window, heavy snow is falling: " 'Snow, snow, snow,' he
repeated senselessly, gazing at the snow which had covered the
fence, the wattled hedge and the beds in the kitchen garden with
a thick layer. 'It has buried everything,' he whispered in despair" (384).

In showing the opposing force acting upon Oblomov from
the beginning of Part III, Goncharov focuses on simple everyday
things, most of which reecho the Oblomovka motifs so master-
fully developed in "Oblomov's Dream." The pastoral surroundings of the summer house where Olga and Oblomov suffered

and rejoiced are replaced by an ambience that seems part barn-
yard, part prison: the "poem of love" is followed by a "physiological sketch."[12] The announcement of Oblomov's arrival in
Vyborg by a flock of cackling hens and a big black dog trying
to break loose and "barking desperately" (IV, 304), recalls the
atmosphere of Oblomovka, with its "ruminating cows, bleating
sheep, and cackling hens" (106). The chained dog is a particularly suggestive leitmotif and recurs regularly until the very end
of the book. The clue to its meaning may be found on the very
last page of "Oblomov's Dream," where several dogs help to
hunt down runaway Ilya. Moreover, Zakhar's response to Oblomov's summons is frequently compared to the "growling of a
chained dog" (11), an image that, with the close relationship
that exists between master and servant, seems relevant also to
the former. The cages of canaries and siskins in Oblomov's new
apartment as well as the many fences in the Vyborg district and
around the Pshenitsyn house, reinforce the sense of confinement.
Oblomov becomes a captive of his atavistic yearning for Oblomovka.

The motif structure of *Oblomov* is worked out with meticulous
care and unerring intuition. In particular, Goncharov shows
great subtlety in associating Oblomov's pipe dreams of Oblomovka with the attractions of life at Vyborg. The keynote is one
of easy gratifications. Thus, while "the paradisal life" includes
a wife and children, Oblomov is not immune to collateral temp-
tations. For example, he imagines a "red-cheeked servant girl
with soft round bare elbows and sunburnt neck" bringing him
dinner as he sprawls on the grass underneath a tree; "the little
rogue drops her eyes and smiles" (IV, 80). Oblomov repeats
this reverie to Stolz with every sensual detail: "sunburnt neck,"
"bare elbows" and the "timidly lowered but arch glance" (186).
The repetitions of this motif of easy love in Part III, especially
the "bare elbows" of his landlady—suitably varied and amplified
by motifs like "bare arms," "high bosom" and others—express
Oblomov's growing fascination with his illicit dream, while Olga
and the idea of marriage recede into the background.

Eventually, the image of the mistress merges with that of the
mother, so that Oblomov's relationship to Agafya acquires a
quasi-incestuous quality.[13] At Oblomovka, essentially a matri-

archy, little Ilya was fed, dressed, and even "educated" by his mother, or by substitute mother figures like the nurse. Life centered on food, and the "clatter of knives" in the kitchen is a dominant motif both in "Oblomov's Dream" and in his reveries about the ideal life; it is also prominent in the Vyborg chapters. Oblomov still likes to be treated like a child; Zakhar even puts on his socks, as his nurse used to do—under protest—many years ago at Oblomovka. Agafya's maternal concern for her gentleman is clearly one of her chief attractions to Oblomov. The landlady's "high bosom, firm as a sofa cushion and never agitated" (IV, 307), has an irresistible fascination for him. Connoting a rudimentary desire, along with the infantile need for a mother's care and an inexorable urge for a life of indolence, this image sums up Oblomov's "dream," "the paradisal life."

The long recapitulation of motifs near the end is a sort of pre-Proustian instance of *temps retrouvé*, by which, like some spiritual Odysseus, Oblomov returns to his beloved Oblomovka, fittingly described by way of a mock-Greek analogy. The *nostos* motif has been kept alive through repeated mention of the contemplated trip to his estate as well as through his favorite reading, travel literature. Curiously, the nostalgic quest of this imaginary traveller seems to succeed: shortly before he dies he concludes that "he had no further to go, nothing more to seek, that the ideal of his life had been fulfilled" (486). His recapture of the Oblomovka past in the St. Petersburg present seems to bear this out. This ironic "fulfilment" without a real quest ties in neatly with the parodistic Hamlet motif, "To move forward or not to move forward," and with the anti-Faust theme which has been discerned by some critics.

The passage of recapture intermingles sensory impressions of Oblomov's Vyborg life with the principal Oblomovka motifs, while the time of his romance—mere history—is passed over. Suspended between sleep and waking, Oblomov falls into a "vague, mysterious state, a sort of hallucination," in which "the present and the past merged and intermingled." In this experience of *déjà vu* the old silence envelops him and he hears "the familiar ticking of the clock and the snap of thread being bitten off." And when he looks at the face of Agafya Matveyevna, who is sewing, "from the depths of his memory there arose a familiar image," clearly that of his mother; for next he sees the drawing room at Oblomovka with his mother and her visitors sewing at the table, while his father paces the floor. Not only has he now—in spirit—returned home, but within his hallucinatory *nostos* there lies an even more gratifying fulfilment, conveyed through a mixture of Biblical and fairy-tale imagery: "He was dreaming he had reached the promised land flowing with milk and honey, where people ate the bread of idleness and were dressed in gold and silver . . ." (IV, 493). And while he listens to the "rattle of plates and the clatter of knives," he hears his nanny's voice pronounce the name "Militrisa Kirbitievna," as she points to Agafya. With his mother, Agafya, and the story-book beauty merging into one, his fairy-tale dream has come true. Then the illusion is broken by the entrance of Stolz.

The breaking of the illusion, as well as Stolz's subsequent rebuke of his friend for his moral dereliction, emphasizes the merely imaginary fulfilment of a mock-*nostos*. Yet, by comparison with Stolz, who like the Zurovs in "The Evil Sickness" flits from one place to another without stop, Oblomov, like Tyazhelenko, acquires a solid presence. Whatever his faults, he has not dissipated his energies by chasing the chimeras of fashion and success; he has simply satisfied the primordial human need for a home, a place to be.

IV *Oblomov and Oblomovism*

Oblomov is one of those relatively few characters in world literature which seem to be virtually inexhaustible in meaning. In his esthetic solidity he yields something to the most varied critical approaches. He is best understood by those who avoid extreme positions. Curiously, one of the extremists was Chekhov, who fairly dismissed him as an "exaggerated figure," a "flabby sluggard";[14] others have seen him as being part of a long tradition of comic lie-abeds. Oblomov is lazy, certainly—Kropotkin calls his reveries "the supreme poetry of laziness"[15]—and he is comic; however, this is saying very little. The substance of Oblomov, however idiosyncratic and "exaggerated," is very real and belongs to his own, as to all time.

Historically, Oblomov derives from romanticism; in a way, he is Goncharov's final judgment on the romantic ethos. Like a romantic hero, Oblomov scorns society and social man, whom he sees as fragmented; he lives in his own world of fantasy; and he suffers from ennui and melancholy, typical manifestations of the *mal du siècle*. Of course, he lacks the energy and striving of a *bona fide* romantic hero. Too, his scorn of society is largely passive, and his dreams are merely tepid idyllic reveries that spur no action. A fragmentary man himself, his name being related to *oblom* or *oblomok*—meaning a "broken piece" or "fragment"—Oblomov would be shattered altogether by the potent ingredients of a genuine romanticism. But however decadent, the romantic element is nonetheless the basis of his character.

This can be shown concretely by comparing him with young Aduev in *A Common Story*. Before his conversion to the gospel of success, Aduev runs through several stages of romanticism: 1) a positive blue-eyed romanticism of the Schillerian type; 2) a negative romanticism of disillusionment à la Byron characterized by spiritual dejection and withdrawal from society; and 3) a stage with a slightly Baudelairean tinge to it that we shall call the "poetry of decay." While *A Common Story* deals mainly with the first of these stages, Oblomov concentrates on the last two. Already in Aduev's case these stages are associated with a lethargic lie-abed existence, an Oblomovesque sleep of the spirit, in the third stage also with an Oriental-type dressing gown (*khalat*). A sort of unregenerate Aduev, Oblomov seems like an answer to one of Belinsky's criticisms of *A Common Story*, namely, that a character like Aduev, a threefold romantic—"by nature, by education, and by circumstances"[16]—could never be cured of his romanticism and had better be left to rot on his estate. We note that, while Oblomov remains physically in the city, psychologically he fulfils Belinsky's requirement: he virtually rots in a hallucinatory Oblomovka.

Oblomov's romance with Olga, who attempts to "resurrect" him, merely hastens the process of decay. His malady is too advanced to allow him to respond actively to her healthy, realistic appeal. For though seen through a romantic haze,[17] Olga is no dreamer. True, as always with Goncharov's young women, her development comes about through emotional experience, but motifs like her habit of frowning and the crease of "con-

centrated thought" over her eye show the dominance of reason
in her make-up. Fond as she may be of Ilya, there is a strong
ideological component in her love, evident both in her reforming
zeal and in her decision to drop him when she realizes he will
never change. Her strict view of life and love as duty is as alien
to Oblomov as are the obligations of marriage that she wishes
him to assume. Neither Olga's charm nor her moral passion can
reconcile Oblomov, with his "poetic dream" of married life, to
its prosaic particulars. The fact that, ultimately, he marries
Agafya is here irrelevant, since his union with her is intrinsically
one of master and servant and, as such, is an aspect of the
"poetry of decay." Olga's idealism as well as its failure acquire
depth through literary allusion. First, with a double twist to a
classical myth, Goncharov makes her into a Pygmalion *manqué*,
in the end unable to breathe life into a male but rather womanish
Galatea; secondly, the failure of Olga's exhortations to Oblomov
to go "higher, higher" (IV, 364) sets up a mocking echo of
Faust: no "Eternal Feminine" can lead Oblomov "upward."

The death of the romantic hero would be a banal theme were
it not used to express specifically Russian realities, in particular
the disintegration of the old indigenous Russian culture and the
primitive natural economy in which it was rooted. However
crude, the culture of Oblomovka was integral; Oblomovkan society corresponds to what sociologists have called *Gemeinschaft,*
a living community based on an organic relationship between
man and nature and, ideally, on relations of personal fealty between master and man. A member of such a community joining
the civilized *Gesellschaft,* in which all pieties have broken down
and relationships between people have become impersonalized,
would be handicapped in much the same way the American
Indian is in our society—and this despite having acquired an
"education." In Oblomov's case, in fact, education is a major
reason for his tragedy, awakening him to the "great gulf between
life and learning" (IV, 66). His experience of boarding school
and university served merely to accumulate whole archives of
dead things, with no relation whatsoever to his life. His way of
thinking and his expectations of life remained those of Oblomovka. Going to work for the government, he expects his department to be a big happy family, with the result that he is

cruelly disappointed and resigns from his post after two years. At the same time, he is also spoiled for Oblomovka. Thus he gets the worst of both worlds: his exposure to European civilization merely accentuates the weaknesses inherent in the old culture, above all its Asiatic quietism, while the Oblomovka mentality with which he is imbued makes history, and civilization itself, look like a never-ending pantomime (64–65). He can only subside into the banal and soulless routine of Vyborg, a petit-bourgeois idyl dominated by semi-ritual events and sharing in the same primordial rhythm as Oblomovka. Doomed by Oblomovism as by the writing on the wall in Belshazzar's Feast (192), he is to be pitied, in the words of Pisarev, as one of the "innocent victims of historical necessity."[18]

The class aspects of Oblomovism, which at first glance may seem the most obvious, are not Goncharov's chief concern; they are important chiefly as far as serfdom is involved. This institution is clearly a main reason for Oblomov's failure. In describing little Ilya's upbringing, Goncharov shows the harmful effects of being catered to by hosts of servants. As Stolz tells Oblomov: "It began with your not knowing how to put on your socks and ended with your not knowing how to live" (IV, 403). Being saturated with the spirit of serfdom, Oblomov in his freedom from work paradoxically becomes the slave of everyone, a point well taken by Dobrolyubov.[19] And, Goncharov suggests, to the extent that the squirearchy allows its life to be determined by the ethos of serfdom, personified by armies of Zakhars, it will be destroyed by the forces of capitalism. In this limited sense, the fate of Oblomov spells the doom of serfdom Russia and of its dominant class, the gentry. But Dobrolyubov was wrong in seeing Oblomov as the so-called "superfluous man" gone to seed, with the implication that the entire gentry intelligentsia was bankrupt. That the author did not think the gentry as a class was finished is evident from his benignly humorous description of an Oblomovesque, but efficient landowner in The Frigate "Pallada," a man who has reconciled the necessity of work with his temperamental predilections through a life of "active indolence and indolent activity" (II, 70). Instead of the gentry's destruction, Goncharov envisaged its revitalization through the bourgeois spirit of the Stolzes.

Moreover, Goncharov plainly suggests that Oblomovism is confined neither to the old autochthonous culture nor to the unprogressive landed gentry. In a discussion with Oblomov, Stolz mentions, besides "rural" Oblomovism, a St. Petersburg variety, defined as gaining "importance and social position through service and afterwards enjoy[ing] a well-earned rest in honorable inactivity" (IV, 189). The jejune dream of the average "educated" Russian of the time, this brand of Oblomovism is equally insidious; its essence is the absence of a genuine purpose and higher values, causing life to be bogged down in materialism and conformity. That Goncharov himself was not unaware of the broader representativeness of his hero is evident from a passage in *Better Late Than Never*, where he writes: ". . . I instinctively felt that the elementary qualities of the Russian were gradually absorbed in this figure . . ." (VIII, 71). Later in the same article he calls Oblomov an "undiluted expression of the masses, reposing in a long and deep sleep" (82). The word "masses" seems to include practically everyone, regardless of class, since in the same paragraph he mentions that nearly all of his acquaintances recognized themselves in Oblomov.

These statements invite the kind of conclusion drawn by Ovsyaniko-Kulikovsky, who saw in Oblomov an image of the "'sickness' of the Russian national psyche." However, he qualifies this by saying that in Oblomovism "the normal Russian ways of thinking and acting received an extreme, hyperbolic expression." If the exaggeration is deducted, we have a "picture of the Russian national psyche."[20] This is "normal" Oblomovism, "expressing itself, in the sphere of will, . . . as inadequate initiative, firmness and perseverance, and in thought by a tendency to fatalistic optimism."[21] Another characteristic is the "absence of a sense of the social value of man."[22] The term "psychological conservatism"[23] used by Kulikovsky is a convenient way of summing up these congeries of allegedly national traits. Interestingly, Lenin seems to have held this broad national interpretation of Goncharov's hero. In a speech made in 1922 he said:

Russia has made three revolutions, and still the Oblomovs have remained, because Oblomov was not only a landowner, but also a peasant; and not only a peasant, but also an intellectual; and not only an intellectual, but also a worker and a Communist. . . . *the old Oblomov has remained, and he must be washed, cleaned, pulled about, and flogged for a long time before any kind of sense will emerge.*[24]

Many critics see Oblomov as a character of broad symbolic reach, expressing problems that concern people everywhere. V. S. Pritchett calls him an "enormous character" who exists on several planes: "Now he seems to symbolize the soul, now he is the folly of idleness, now he is the accuser of success."[25] Mostly these larger meanings are explicated in the light of a particular philosophy or psychological theory. Thus, L. Ganchikov, from an existentialist perspective, sees Oblomov's predicament to consist in an irreconcilable conflict between the human spirit and the indifference of the world, more oppressive in Russia than elsewhere because of its vast size. "The torment of consciousness at being unable to give a truly absolute significance to life, while it cannot resign itself to the relative values— this is what *Oblomov* profoundly expresses."[26] In this perspective Oblomov becomes almost a symbol of the human soul imprisoned in matter and consciously refusing to pay homage to the uses of this world. Such a view, however, has only a limited validity. True, Oblomov does refuse to play the game and join the rat race; he also stands up for integral man and deplores the fragmentation of people in a society which is becoming more and more an arena for the Stolzes of this world. But though his situation and, partly, his ideas can be defined within the existentialist context, his attitude cannot. For instead of choosing to keep the flame of life burning because life is short, as Stolz urges him to do, he prefers to go to sleep forever (IV, 402–3). Indeed, apart from certain idealizing tendencies that are out of key with the general tone of a study in decay, Oblomov sinks deeper and deeper into a mediocre anonymity, what Heidegger calls *das Man.* Spiritually atrophied, Oblomov refuses to confront the human condition in full consciousness.

The psychoanalytical approach seems more pertinent. Shorn of their philosophical frills, Oblomov's absolute spiritual demands become an instance of "infantile omnipotence."[27] It is certainly possible to view not only Oblomov's sexual backwardness and his entropic leaning toward Agafya, but also his dream of attaining the lost paradise, the emphasis on wholeness and so forth, as manifestations of a deep yearning to return to the womb,[28] a death wish. The great theme of Goncharov's *oeuvre*, according to Leon Stilman, is the stages of man's life: infancy, adolescence, adulthood; the key issue is moving from one stage to another and being able, or not being able, to make the transitions successfully. Oblomov refuses to make these transitions; instead he regresses to his childhood, and his death, Stilman writes, suggests a "return to the darkness and peace of the prenatal universe."[29] Thus, Oblomov is seen as a "neurotic personality of a century ago."[30] While removing the odium of neurosis, Milton A. Mays also appeals to psychoanalysis. In his archetypal interpretation of Oblomov, the latter emerges as an embodiment of Freud's ego or death instinct, as opposed to Faust, the expression of the sexual or life instinct.[31] Neither of these views invalidates the socio-historical meaning of the novel, the best works of art uniting the universal and the particular. The dynamics of the *id* may acquire historical significance if a great intuitive artist looks deep enough into himself and his age to make a creative synthesis.

However Oblomov is interpreted, some part of him will resist rationalization. No explication of Oblomovism can explain why Oblomov is an attractive figure for whom we feel a deep sympathy. It is hardly just because he bears the burden of our secret inclinations, toward laziness, social indifference and provisional living, or that, as V. S. Pritchett puts it, he is the expression of our "underwater self."[32] Nor is an appeal to his good qualities, his gentleness and residual nobility, to the point. The gilded phrases of Stolz—an "honest faithful heart," a soul "translucent, clear as crystal," a man who would never "bow down to false idols" (IV, 480–81)—are equally irrelevant. Stolz's eulogy, pronounced *before* Oblomov's death, is no less flattering than most eulogies: Goncharov's beloved hero committed all the sins that Stolz acquits him of. Despite his indifference to society, he is a weak conformist; all his life he respected shams. And he was anything but faithful to Olga; in fact, he "betrayed" her. Assuming that Stolz speaks for the author, the idealizing trend in the passage shows a kind of dichotomy between Goncharov the thinker and the artist. As a thinker he is bound by the traditional psychology and uses terms like "soul" and "heart" to signify unchanging essences, while as artist, in describing Oblomov's actual behavior, he dispenses with such preconceptions. No exception is made for Oblomov's "heart," "soul," or faithfulness when, during one of Stolz's visits, we watch him get drunk on home-made currant vodka and "greedily" attack the mutton. Meanwhile he constantly praises Agafya: Olga, he says, may sing "Casta diva," "but she can't make vodka like this!" (449) This is the real Oblomov. In order to discover his virtues, we must know the pitiless truth about him.

The truth is that Oblomov is a study in decay, of a maimed life. Oblomov says himself that, unlike other lives, his never knew a dawn which gradually became a "blazing day," to wane slowly into the "evening twilight." His life, he says, "began in extinction." In a sentence that sounds like an unwitting parody of the Cartesian *cogito*, Oblomov continues: "From the very moment I became conscious of myself, I felt that I was expiring" (IV, 190), which could be paraphrased as follows: I think, therefore, I am not. His habit of watching the sunset is a symbolic expression of this feeling. One is reminded of the naturalistic tendency to stress the descending phase of the life cycle, along with the mind's and the heart's dependence upon the ceaselessly changing body. Steeped in matter, Oblomov is no Daedalus to take wing above a sea of trouble, to vary Goncharov's own imagery; even the loftiest feeling generates only a brief arc of flight, the longest being that of his romance. And afterwards he falls into a more hopeless morass than ever. When Stolz on his last visit urges him to get "out of this pit, this bog, into the light," he answers: "I have grown bodily into this pit; if you try to tear me out it will be my death" (496).

We seem to have arrived at the commonplace appeal of "a world I never made," which can only scratch the surface of our feeling for Oblomov. The key to that feeling lies in his arrested development. Goncharov's maimed hero, lacking the adult adaptation to real life, is by compensation endowed with certain qualities that evoke a nostalgic empathy. He is childlike, feminine, androgynous. After Penkin's departure he "rejoiced that he lay as carefree as a newborn babe" (IV, 31); his loves "were as innocent, simple, and pure as the love stories of a boarding school girl" (62); and his body "seemed too delicate for a man" (8). Moreover, he demands both from Zakhar and from Olga a loyalty and love as absolute as the one a child demands from its mother. His inability to meet the challenge of a young girl's love is reminiscent of Prince Myshkin in Dostoevsky's *The Idiot*. These two characters are also alike in other ways. Both are nonviolent, nonacquisitive men beloved of all, but inviting evil by their passive goodness; easy victims, they attract evil parasites who encroach upon their moral space.[33] Yet, to speak of Oblomov, his very weakness acquires a positive value, associated as it is with images of pure potentiality. Apart from those that have been mentioned, the image of paralysis recalls Oblomov's great namesake, the Russian *bogatyr* Ilya Muromets, who entered upon his hero's mission in his early thirties after being cured of actual paralysis. There is in Oblomov, who at the outset of the story has reached Ilya Muromets' critical age, the seed of something great; however lost, he keeps a rich treasure buried in his soul, "hidden like gold in the depths of a mountain"; though he may be to blame for not putting it "into circulation" (100–101), it is undeniably there, like the core of a second, undeveloped self. This is the basis of Goncharov's love of his hero, despite his severe judgment of him. It also justifies that very moving moment of communion in which Oblomov posthumously unites Olga, Stolz, and Agafya (503). And it is the basis of our own ability to identify with this tragicomic figure, whose unlived life—symbolized by the lilac—must strike a responsive chord in every man.

V   *Stolz and Stolzism*

The alternative to Oblomov and Oblomovism presented in a subplot is singularly unattractive, and its representative, Stolz, has not been kindly treated by the critics. Most unfavorable, perhaps, was the opinion of the reviewer for *The Russian Messenger*, quipping that Stolz was not born of a father and mother, but as an "ideal antithesis." He goes on to call him Oblomov's Mephistopheles, his "paradoxical and misplaced double." And, he says, since an abstraction tends toward the thing it is abstracted from, Stolz "tends toward Oblomovism, despite the contrast."[34] Orest Miller later called him "an eternally moving Oblomov." Since his ambition stops at material well-being, his life, Miller comments, is essentially "empty, deprived of any higher aims and in this sense Oblomovesque, or even lower; for Oblomov feels the emptiness of his life, while Stolz smugly plunges into his."[35] Even Goncharov joined the chorus of criticism. In a letter of 1860 addressed to the Nikitenko sisters, he takes a contemptuous attitude toward Stolz (VIII, 329), and in *Better Late Than Never* he writes: "He is weak, pale—the idea stands out too baldly" (80). As compared to these criticisms, Dobrolyubov's main objection, namely, that Stolz cannot utter the word "Forward!"[36] is mild indeed.

A kind of Sir Charles Grandison of Russian literature, Andrey Stolz sums up all the perfections of man. While down-to-earth and practical, he is also an idealist; he combines the qualities of a businessman with the refinements of high intellectual culture. His programmatic quality is most evident from his heredity and social milieu. Whereas Oblomov is the product of one single environment, which dyed him in the wool and held him captive for life, Stolz is the composite creation of several: his social inheritance ranges from the petit-bourgeois world of his plebeian father, an estate steward, to the aristocratic elegancies of the Prince's mansion, with Oblomovka somewhere in between.

Goncharov stresses the variety of his social experience; as he grew up, Andrey "with his childish green eyes looked at three or four different social circles at once, and with his quick mind eagerly and unconsciously watched the different types of this heterogeneous crowd . . ." (IV, 163). The multiple milieu also reaches into his home, where the social inequalities between a Russian lady and a German *Bürger* are compounded by national differences. The intermingling of all these traditions and milieus is presumably the key to the harmonious development of Stolz, whose names—Andrey, derived from the Greek *anér, andrós*, "man," and Stolz, German for "pride"—mark him as the expression of a humanist ideal. Accordingly, the mother's fear that he might become a commonplace and pedantic German is groundless: "The German element was confronted on the one hand by Oblomovka, on the other by the Prince's castle with its manorial life of ease and opulence, and Andrey did not grow up to be either a good *Bursch,* or even a Philistine" (164). The German element merely provided the groundwork of the structure, while Russia allegedly gave it life and beauty.

A result of cross-cultural breeding, the "bourgeois" hero of Goncharov, therefore, is conceived as anything but the representative of a single class, or even a single country; he represents an idea. It is true that, through Stolz, the author claims to have expressed a real historical fact, namely, the great importance of the German contribution to Russian civilization. "The best and richest branches of industry, commercial and other enterprises are in their hands," he writes (VIII, 81). But over and above his deference to social dynamics, one senses a cultural ideal. More than a Russified German of mixed background, Stolz is the epitome of a vigorous cosmopolitan civilization as opposed to the decadent autochthonous culture of Oblomovka. Interestingly, Goncharov ends his discussion of Stolz in *Better Late Than Never* with a statement that in the future the Slavophiles, while preserving the Russian spirit, will "sincerely hold out their hands to universal, that is European, culture; for if feelings and convictions are national, knowledge is one everywhere and for all" (82).

Even Oblomov finds a place within this grand design. To Stolz, Oblomov is inseparably associated with warm feelings of home, childhood and his native land, and the famous sofa is a welcome haven to him (IV, 171–72). Ultimately, Goncharov's multicultural concept, a sort of cross-fertilization of subcultures, is predicated on a harmonious synthesis of indigenous and foreign, gentry and bourgeois, conservatism and progress. None of the various strands which make up the texture of Russian culture and determine the Russian character is entirely rejected, whether the "ideal stillness" of Oblomovka or the quasi-Faustian streak in Stolz; both must be subsumed within the new national identity. The hope for such a synthesis, which seems quite impossible to a sober mind, may be the only *raison d'être* of Andrey Oblomov, Oblomov's son, whose name unites those of two opposites.

Here, however, we are dealing with intangibles: the highest synthesis is merely a hint.[37] What really is at stake is the idea represented by Stolz. Whatever this idea may be worth, the author did not succeed in making either Andrey or Olga Stolz believable characters. Partly this may be due to the nature of his work, which could hardly contain another world of equal density to Oblomov's. Secondly, the very idea of an ideal character causes strain and artificiality. When, for example, we read that Stolz lived "according to a set plan and tried to spend each day as he spent each ruble, keeping a firm and unremitting watch over the expenditure of his time, his labor, and his mental and emotional powers" and that he "seemed to govern his joys and sorrows like the movements of his hands and feet" (IV, 167–68), we are struck by a sense of unconscious burlesque. Much worse, however, is the fact that, once married, he also totally "governs" Olga, while their much vaunted love comes to seem a mirage.

Regrettably, Olga Stolz is several rungs below Olga Ilinsky. Whereas the latter is a lively, intelligent, and mildly ironic young lady of enlightened views, the former is dull and conformist. Olga's decline is evident already in Switzerland, where she acts like a real ninny. On account of her inconclusive romance with Oblomov, the girl who, through that romance, supposedly entered "the realm of consciousness" (IV, 235) and who has a "correct understanding of true, sincere, and independent morality" (418), treats herself as a "fallen" woman, an attitude which places Stolz in the position of a noble rescuer. And despite her natural vivacity, their life together bears his imprint: "Like a thinker and an artist he was weaving a rational existence for her" (467). Goncharov was apparently aware of the change in her character. In a letter of August 14, 1857, he writes that, at first, Olga was simple and natural, but then seemingly "fell apart" (VIII, 292). Only at the end of the last scene with Stolz (Pt. IV, ch. 8) do we again glimpse the former strong-willed, stubborn Olga, though she has lost her old charm.

The chief weakness of Goncharov's handling of the Olga-Stolz relationship is his imposition of an ideal scheme which, on examination, turns out to be hollow or, worse, a mask for a drab reality. We are told in extolling tones that "nothing was done without her knowledge or participation. Not a single letter was sent without first reading it to her, not a single idea, still less its realization, was kept from her; she knew everything, and everything interested her because it interested him" (IV, 466). But what is this except the complete triumph of the worst side of Stolzism: conceived as a model of mutual equality, the ideal marriage has turned into a business partnership, the epitome of Philistinism. This is also the basis on which Olga judges her husband, solely by his worth, as one estimates the value of a piece of property, or a commodity. "Having once recognized the worth of the man she had chosen and his claims upon her, she believed in him and therefore loved him, and if she ceased to believe she would also cease to love . . ." (477). Stolz's anxious fears before his proposal that "she submitted to him consciously," whereas "in love merit is acquired blindly, without any conscious reason," with the inference that "it is in this very blindness and unconsciousness that happiness lies" (415), are therefore fully justified.

Probably against his will, Goncharov has suggested the artistic truth, namely, that Olga does not love Stolz and that, despite her contemptuous sneer at Oblomov's capacity for "tenderness" in the moment of parting from him (IV, 382), she has always retained a warm affection for him. Deep within her heart she does not go along with Stolz's attempt, following Oblomov's lead in his frantic letter to Olga, to reduce her feelings for him to mere illusion. For that matter, their own family life —the children, her difficult confinements and all—is little better than illusory, and Goncharov is less than credible in portraying Olga's feelings toward her husband. One evening during a long conversation she "threw herself into his [Stolz's] arms like one possessed and, clasping her arms around his neck like a bacchante, stood still for a moment in passionate self-abandonment" (475). Instead of passion there is a convulsion. This outburst, in conjunction with Goncharov's candid exposition of Olga's "strange malady" (470), suggests that the underlying cause of Olga's recurrent attacks of depression is a deep erotic frustration.

Though forestalling a sexual interpretation, Goncharov at the same time invites it. For the conversation just referred to, taking place on a walk in a poplar avenue, reechoes the "hot and sultry" evening with Oblomov and another walk down a tree-lined avenue. Pathological terms like "morbid symptoms," "mysterious attack," and others are either used or implied in both instances, and some of Olga's gestures recur. Since the "morbid symptoms" of Olga in the first scene are clearly sexual in origin, her malaise as a married woman may be assumed to stem from similar causes. This is hardly surprising considering her husband's well-regulated character. Moreover, her discontent is also moral and psychological. She is clearly irked by an egocentric streak in her husband's make-up, as when he complains of the trouble that Oblomov has given him, and Olga seems to prefer the prospect of any privation and disaster to their unadventurous mundane life. He never succeeded in filling the "whole depth of her soul" (IV, 464). What emerges is a recurrence of the predicament of Peter Aduev and Lizaveta, and like the latter, Olga, the "soul" of the novel in the author's words (VIII, 285), is the touchstone of both male characters. But it is as if Goncharov tries to hide this insight, which comes to us by surreptitious and seemingly unconscious hints and allusions. For consciously, as a thinker, the author tries to resolve Olga's problem philosophically.

With misplaced consistency the author connects Olga's malaise with Oblomovism, in the sense of being steeped in an existence without meaning and purpose. To judge by the fact that the motifs recalled at Stolz's engagement to Olga are all associated with gentry life (IV, 435), as well as by the statement that they lived "like everyone else, and as Oblomov had dreamed" (465), the basis of their way of life is that of the landed gentry; however, it is allegedly enriched both with bourgeois features and such as are associated with the liberal intelligentsia. Nevertheless, Olga is "afraid of sinking into an apathy like Oblomov's." But whereas Oblomov's apathy is a priori, so to speak, hers is a posteriori, a result of having experienced whatever happiness life can offer. She is faced with the thorny Tolstoyan question so memorably dramatized through Levin in *Anna Karenina*. The closed "circle of life" leaves her unsatisfied, and nature is in league with the great god boredom: it "said the same thing over and over again; she saw in it the endless, monotonous flow of life without beginning or end" (469).

As presented by Goncharov, the problem faced by Olga is bound to emerge wherever nature is demythologized, causing ritual to be replaced by routine. In such a context consciousness becomes isolated from total being and starts challenging life itself. Stolz says: "A lively searching mind . . . sometimes strives to go beyond the boundaries of life and finding, of course, no answers, becomes melancholy . . . temporarily dissatisfied with life . . . It is the melancholy of the soul questioning life about its mysteries." Then he speaks eloquently about her feeling of bitterness in the midst of happiness as "what one has to pay for the Promethean fire!" These doubts and questions, he says, are the "surplus, the luxury of life, and mostly appear on the summits of happiness when there are no coarse desires; they do not arise in ordinary life: those in need and sorrow cannot be bothered with them" (IV, 474). We recognize this theme as a variant of the Hamletic tragedy of mind, whereby pure consciousness, its organic relations with nature and society severed, reduces life to a "weary, stale, flat, and unprofitable" routine.

Goncharov's handling of this theme, which could be called the Oblomovism of the élite, is hardly satisfactory. The allusion to "Promethean fire" would seem to strike a heroic note, a challenge to the gods and the status quo; but soon Stolz is feeding Olga the pabulum of traditional wisdom. "You and I are not Titans," he says, to "struggle defiantly with insoluble questions"; instead, he tells her, "we shall . . . bow our heads and humbly live through the difficult time . . ." (IV, 475). Then, again, he strikes a slightly more affirmative, "modern" note. Though these questions, Stolz says, "bring us to an abyss from which we can get no answer, . . . they challenge well-tried forces to do battle with them, as if on purpose not to let them go to sleep" (474). The implication, reminiscent of an existentialist idea, is that the sense of life, as of love and consciousness, is heightened by the glance into the abyss.

The wavering attitude suggests that some of this is mere rhetoric. In fact, Goncharov frequently succumbs to the facile allure of rhetoric in describing Stolz's education of Olga. He speaks of "the fire with which he lighted the cosmos" he created for her, of the "fruitful drop" of his talk sinking, "like a pearl, into the limpid depths of her being" (IV, 467), and of entering the "labyrinth of her mind and character" with the "torch of experience" (413). This pretentious imagery confirms our suspicion of Stolz, who fails to project a clearly realized *Weltanschauung*. Moreover, the whole situation is marked by unreality, despite Stolz's indirect assertion, in saying that the "common malady" of mankind is "frightening [only] when one has lost touch with life" (475), that his and Olga's life is solidly anchored in the real. Such an assertion is meaningless unless the author proves it by a convincing character portrayal, and this kind of proof is toward the end of the novel offered only by Oblomov and Agafya. Seemingly, Goncharov is at this point esthetically schizoid, switching back and forth between the extremes of subjective and objective art. While the presumably rich, vibrant, and fully conscious life of the Stolzes is, in effect, just a bag of dry bones, the dull, monotonous, and virtually unconscious existence of Oblomov and Agafya is very much alive. This is the central paradox of Goncharov's art. Significantly, the Vyborg sections, even where general narrative is used, create distinctive moods ranging from burlesque humor to pathos, while the description of the Stolzes—prize exhibits for a positive philosophy—lacks a distinctive emotional coloring.

VI   *Goncharov's Comic-Epic Vision in* Oblomov

In *Oblomov* Goncharov shows great artistic versatility. As might be expected from a prose writer who began with burlesque, he is a master of the comic, especially the mock-heroic variety; but at the same time he is a great lyric poet in prose, as shown by his "love poem" (*poema liubvi*), a term he applies to the Oblomov-Olga romance. He displays veritable genius for what we have called the "poetry of decay," a loving portrayal of the process of disintegration. Together with his epic sweep in encompassing the life of an entire culture in "Oblomov's Dream," as well as his gift for minute observation, this constitutes an impressive array of talents. One notes that every one of these talents is directed toward the existing world, whether to expose, celebrate, or simply paint it. When, however, he leaves the actual for the ideal, he becomes much too abstract and rhetorical. In this respect he is the antithesis of a writer like Dostoevsky, most of whose great characters are "ideal" in the esthetic sense; but though based on a *Weltanschauung* or even an ideology, they have an almost terrifying reality.

All of Goncharov's talents come to full fruition in *Oblomov*. Whereas previously, for example, his comedy is largely situational, now he creates a great comic figure. We recall how in his early work humor is produced through juxtaposing incongruous perspectives, romantic and utilitarian; now it derives chiefly from incongruities within the world of the central character. The basic formula is the tension between the dreams, fancies and visions of a contemplative mind, and a body dominated by inertia and crude physical need. Thus, while showing Oblomov impassioned by heroic zeal to expose the evil in the world—his thoughts surge "like ocean waves" and "set his blood on fire"— Goncharov subtly reminds the reader of the physical fact of a body in bed: "impelled by a moral force, he rapidly changed his position two or three times within one minute . . ." (IV, 69). Again, in the very heat of his decision to rise and order his affairs, Oblomov's sentences suddenly dribble away. His arms relaxing and his knees giving way, he yawns and thinks of food. Extended use of this technique produces effects that verge on psychological incoherence, a comic version of the split personality. " 'Yes, there's plenty to do,' he said softly. 'Take the plan alone—lots of work still to be done on it! . . . But there certainly was some cheese left,' he added thoughtfully. 'Zakhar has eaten it, and now he says there wasn't any' " (82). The image of Oblomov is produced by such shifts from the serious to the ludicrous, while his "fate" is incongruously decided by such things as an insect bite, a pair of elbows, rich pies, and home-made brandy. Into the gaps between these extremes, laughter inserts itself, sometimes tinged with irony or pathos, but mostly humorous.

Occasionally, the author rises beyond psychological incongruities to cosmic ones. Oblomov's convalescence is seen against the background of the slow erosion of a mountain and the rise and recession of the sea; then these natural phenomena become metaphors of human events: "The gradual raising or lowering of the sea bed and the crumbling away of the mountain was going on in all of them . . ." (IV, 388). When Goncharov conveys Agafya's falling in love with Oblomov by way of these

phenomena, supplemented by "slight volcanic eruptions" (389),
his vision is reminiscent of that of Joyce, who places Molly
and Leopold Bloom in relation to the stellar universe. Like
Joyce, Goncharov uses shifting camera angles and distances.
Thus, Oblomov's stroke is first viewed as part of a cosmic order,
the proximate causes—his indolence and gluttony—being presented later. The shocks of life reach even that quiet little
corner, Goncharov says, just as a "thunderclap that shakes the
foundations of mountains and vast aerial spaces is also heard
in a mousehole—less loudly and strongly, it is true, but still
quite perceptibly" (488). Then follows a description of Oblomov's routine of easy living and hard eating and drinking.
Curiously, the effect of placing the characters within this rigorous
framework of sea and rock and of comparing them to animals
and plants, is anything but chilling; on the contrary, it is in
such moments that the author seems to love them most. Softened
by Goncharov's cosmic humor, warm and all-encompassing, the
absorption of their lives within this framework confers a humble
dignity upon them.

These techniques reflect a definite sense of life, best defined
perhaps by the word "epic." An equable temper rules in the
world of Goncharov, where potentially shattering events such
as love, passion, and death are treated as ordinary occurrences.
The homely image of the "stream of life" appears not only in
the description of Oblomovka; the calm sense of existence it
connotes is shared by characters as dissimilar as Oblomov and
Stolz. Proposing to Olga, Oblomov only momentarily longed for
"tears, passion, intoxicating happiness . . . ; afterwards life could
flow on in unruffled calm!" (IV, 294). And Stolz, the author
says, "did not want violent passion any more than Oblomov";
he merely wanted it to "surge up hotly at the source" before
it settled into its "even stream" (417). The "stream" image
tends to occur also in "summary moments" where a character
discovers his place in life. After accepting Stolz, Olga felt as
if he had taken her "not into a brilliant, dazzling light but, as
it were, to a broad, overflowing river, to wide fields and friendly,
smiling hills. . . . Her gaze rested with quiet joy on the broad
stream of life, on its vast fields and green hills" (435).

While deflating elements of drama and passion, Goncharov's epic manner is no hindrance to a sympathetic understanding of little things and people. This is most evident in the story of Agafya, which to some extent parallels that of Oblomov. For, at a lower level, Oblomov offers her what Olga had offered him: a chance to wake up and realize herself as an individual. However, once awakened, Agafya never entirely reverts to her previous torpor. The low-keyed description of the vicissitudes of her love for Oblomov, which causes her to grow thin or plump depending upon the gentleman's attitude toward her (IV, 390), is one of the highpoints of Goncharov's humane realism, capable of investing the lowliest and most bovine existence with meaning. "In her own way she began to live a full and varied life" (391). Through her humble role as Oblomov's housekeeper her life is transfigured and his death means a new initiation.

> Before her husband's body . . . she seemed suddenly to have grasped the meaning of her life and to have grown thoughtful, and ever since this thoughtfulness lay like a shadow over her face. . . . She realized that . . . the sunshine that had illumined . . . [her life] was darkened forever . . . ; but her life had been given meaning forever, too. (502)

The most inarticulate existences find esthetic redemption in Goncharov.

VII *Archetypal and Other Imagery in* Oblomov

The epic vision does not, however, monopolize Goncharov's art; the latter also takes in areas of experience which transcend the organic, evoking them through appropriate imagery. In particular, Goncharov expresses both the ecstasy and the torment of love, using images of music and light, as well as such archetypal ones as heaven and hell.

Though firmly placed within its natural setting, the "poem of love" reaches beyond it toward an ideal realm. It does so mainly through a consistent use of visual and auditory imagery, unified by a musical analogy of theme and variations. This analogy seems a fitting extension of the inspiration of Oblomov's love, namely, Olga's singing of "Casta diva" from Bellini's opera

Norma, a motif initially associated with Oblomov's dream of
an earthly paradise (IV, 186). The scheme is set out in the
following passage:

Thus the same theme was played by them in different variations. Their
meetings, their conversations—it was all one song, one melody, one bright
light refracted . . . into rays of rose, green, and amber which shimmered in
the surrounding atmosphere. Each day and hour brought new sounds and
colors, but the light and the theme were the same. (253)

Then, as love seems to turn into duty after their secret
betrothal, it begins to "lose its rainbow tints. That morning,
perhaps, he had caught its last roseate rays, and from now on
it would no longer shine so brightly, but warm his life un-
seen. . . . The poem of love was over and stern reality was
beginning" (301–2).

Implicitly, the organic image of heat and the more esthetically
stirring sound and color imagery express the prose and the
poetry of love, respectively. The combination of these images
suggests an ideal harmony of body and spirit. Oblomov is
incapable of achieving this harmony. In his relationship with
Olga he tends to alternate between one extreme and another,
rarely attaining a sense of plenitude. Only in a last euphoric
moment a couple of days before the breakup does he feel both
the poetry and the comfort of love: "he had warmth and light—
and how good life was then!" (IV, 365). His connection with
Agafya is by the imagery firmly placed within the prose of
life: "He drew nearer to Agafya Matveyevna as one does to a
fire which makes one feel warmer and warmer, but which
cannot be loved" (394). On the other hand, Agafya's love,
said at one time to be without "the play and music of the
nerves" (391), is retrospectively completed by the missing part;
after Oblomov's death she "realized that her life had had its
music and its radiance" (502). And though the love of Stolz
and Olga is deliberately conveyed in antiromantic, "epic" imagery, such as a tree "spreading its branches over the whole
of life" (462), "broad wings" (436) or a protective shadow
(465), Goncharov means their love to unite heat and light in
ideal synthesis. He speaks several times of Stolz's fire and

brilliance and, more subtly, makes Olga at her betrothal to him fix her mental gaze on the "blue still night, warm, fragrant, and with a gently shimmering radiance" (436). By contrast, Olga's feeling for Oblomov is compared to a "false flame, a light without heat" (259). Though slightly artificial, this use of imagery to set up a standard of perfect love is less obtrusive than other attempts to present the ideal in Goncharov's fiction.

The imagery of love often merges with archetypal concepts of heaven, hell, and earthly paradise. Olga, whose face makes Oblomov feel as though he is looking into an "infinite distance or a bottomless abyss" (IV, 206) and who "liked the role of guiding star" (239), is an Eve with a perceptible streak of Beatrice in her. Oblomov constantly imagines Olga as belonging to a different, higher sphere, which occasionally gives him the sensation of flying. More frequently, however, he despairs of attaining this sphere, seeing Olga as a "pure angel" soaring above the "abyss," at the bottom of which he envisages himself (258); or a Tarantiev may, "in an instant," bring him "down from heaven, as it were, into the bog again" (297). These images are not without a realistic basis in his experience: they are the dreamlike exaggerations of the fearful ravine—supposedly swarming with all sorts of horrors—that little Ilya was not allowed to approach.[38] The region of the unknown, and of his undeveloped self, becomes his hell; for both abyss and bog are appropriate images of hell. Moreover, "bog" and its variants bear closely upon Oblomov's particular failings. The marsh called Styx which forms the fifth circle of Dante's *Inferno* accommodates the souls of those who were gloomy-sluggish:

> Fixed in the slime, they say: "Sullen were we
> in the sweet air, that is gladdened by the sun,
> carrying lazy smoke within our hearts;
> now lie we sullen here in the black mire."[39]

After Olga's visit at his Vyborg lodgings, Oblomov thinks of her as an angel descending into a "bog" (*boloto*, with the figurative meaning of "mire"). And Stolz speaks about Oblomov in the same terms, telling him that "if an angel like Olga could not carry you out of the bog on her wings, then I can do nothing" (401).

The idea of an earthly paradise, which received a new lease on life through Romanticism, plays a significant role in the book. Oblomov implicitly defines his goal as attaining the "lost paradise" (IV, 187), conceived as a rustic idyl with submissive peasants and even more submissive peasant girls, and he envisages himself with Olga "in his earthly paradise, Oblomovka" (224). But his dream of escape to an ivory tower of love finds its ironic fulfilment in the Vyborg district, a "bog" of low pleasures in which Oblomov's spirit nearly chokes to death. The vulnerability of the dream is early suspected by Olga; even before their secret engagement she would occasionally sink into an "oppressive reverie: something cold as a snake crept into her heart, wakening her from her dream, and the warm fairy-tale world of love turned into a gray autumn day" (282). Here, as in every earthly paradise, the proverbial serpent lurks around the corner.

The use of this traditional imagery, which may or may not have been suggested by Dante, does not necessarily imply a Christian *Weltanschauung*; in fact, Goncharov seems closer to Greek humanism than to Christianity. The "wing" image, for example, connotes something like self-motivation. "You had wings once, but you took them off," Stolz tells Oblomov. "You lost your ability to do things when still a child at Oblomovka, among your aunts and nurses" (IV, 403). The paralysis of the will, abulia, which afflicts Oblomov is not rooted in original sin and is beyond redemption. Whatever its ultimate cause, it is surely connected with Oblomov's self-confessed lack of pride (218), quite distinct from Christian humility. According to Stolz, pride (*samoliubie*) is "almost the only motivating force that controls the will" (207); consequently, it is a positive moral force. It is not for pride as such but for *excess* of pride, on account of her singlehanded endeavor to arouse the pride of life in Oblomov, that Olga—Greek fashion—is "punished." There is nothing in Goncharov's use of Christian archetypes that conflicts with this humanistic bias. Moreover, the context in which they appear invites a psychological rather than a religious interpretation: they are chiefly a means of evoking the dreamy, anguished inner world of Oblomov, whose point of view justifies the most exalted rhetoric.

VIII *Goncharov's Inspiration*

Goncharov is a very "literary" writer, absorbing ideas and images from a wide variety of sources, but by the time he wrote *Oblomov* his borrowings are so transformed that one can hardly speak of literary "influences" in the ordinary sense. The only exception may be Gogol, whose story "Old-time Land-owners" had inspired Goncharov's first idea for a novel, "The Old People" (*Stariki*). Though the novel was never written, *Oblomov* includes a masterly treatment of the same theme; however, the center of gravity is no longer manners and everyday life, but psychological portraiture. Because of this shift, specific counterparts to Oblomov in Gogol's work, such as Manilov, Tentetnikov, and Platonov in *Dead Souls,* bear only a superficial likeness to Goncharov's character.[40] Moreover, long before *Dead Souls* was published, an Oblomovesque figure had been realized in Tyazhelenko, the gluttonous sloth of "The Evil Sickness" (1838). Thus, while Goncharov is "literary" in the sense that he freely assimilates devices, themes, and even imagery from other writers, the basis of his work, as he says himself in *Better Late Than Never,* was his own experience and the observation of his contemporaries.

This fact is strongly supported by his recollections in "At Home" ("Na rodine"), which presents vignettes of the sleepy town of Simbirsk and of local gentry life. From his childhood the author, then seventy-five, recalls how Yakubov—actually Tregubov, his godfather—and his gentlemen friends used to lie in bed practically all day: "It seems to me that already then, at the sight of all these figures, this carefree life, idleness and lying around, there arose in me, a very sharp-eyed and impressionable boy, a vague idea of 'Oblomovism'." And when he returned to Simbirsk in 1834, he was surrounded by the same "Oblomovism" which he had observed in childhood. "The very appearance of my native town presented nothing else than a picture of sleep and stagnation." Interestingly, the details are reminiscent of the St. Petersburg suburb where Oblomov ends up. The houses were "surrounded by ditches, thickly overgrown with wormwood and nettles," and there were "endless fences" (VII, 242). One felt like going to sleep, he writes, just

looking at this calm, at the sleepy countenances of those sitting around
in the houses or of the people you run into in the street. 'We have nothing
to do!' each of these people seems to think, yawning and looking lazily
at us; 'we are not in a hurry, we live—we chew our bread and idle our
life away.' (243)

Goncharov's septuagenarian recollections are quite prosaic;
the memory which operates here is largely factual. In his novel,
on the other hand, emotive memory imbues with poetry the
sleepy world that he had observed. The source of this poetry,
as well as of the vividness and undeniable charm of his hero,
is no doubt the author's intimacy with "Oblomovs" from his
childhood. Little Vanya loved Tregubov with all his lying around,
and Ivan Goncharov, the author, loves his Oblomov, whose
chronic idleness is more attractive than Stolz's fussy activity.
And though the story of Oblomov seems to be offered as a
caveat—"it may be of use to someone" (IV, 507), Stolz tells the
stand-in for the author at the end of the novel—it has a bitter-
sweet beauty, nostalgic but serene, which is extremely alluring.
Love-laden "branches of lilac . . . drowse over his grave," tem-
pering the "scent of wormwood" in the still air (499). The lesson
we may forget, or not need; but the bizarre, somewhat decadent
loveliness of Oblomov's tragicomic figure will always haunt the
reader of Goncharov's masterpiece.

CHAPTER 5

The Precipice

GONCHAROV's last novel was conceived in 1849 on a visit to Simbirsk, his native town, but was published only twenty years later. The delay in completing the work was partly due to the distractions of service and the prior claim of *Oblomov;* less obvious reasons were connected with the nature of his talent and the contemporary literary scene. Endowed with an extraordinary gift for observation and precise description, Goncharov had a weak structural imagination and his creative process often lacked direction. Much like his artist-hero Raysky in *The Precipice,* he would sketch isolated scenes, characters, and settings with only the vaguest idea as to how they were to be integrated. The spark which triggered the unifying conception was slow in coming, dependent upon the imponderables of personal experience. In the writing of *Oblomov* the breakthrough occurred when the romance with Olga assumed concrete shape under the influence of Goncharov's unhappy wooing of Elizabeth Tolstoy. As for *The Precipice,* several stages are apparent in its genesis. However, in order fully to understand the changes in the author's plan one must have a general notion of the finished work.

Boris Raysky, a gentry intellectual living in St. Petersburg, is a genteel Bohemian with a knack for art and a taste for amour. Now in his mid-thirties, his talent is still undeveloped because of indolence and a romantic concept of art. A dilettante, he flits from one art to another or practices them all together; painting, music, and literature become merely stages on the way to his "true" vocation: sculpture. Though Raysky is in dead earnest, these recurrences make his passion for art some-

115

what suspect. The same applies to the parallel quest for the perfect woman, which turns him into a sort of Russian Don Juan. However, by blending Don Juanism with an all but Hamletic penchant for self-scrutiny Goncharov produces a nearly schizoid type whose pursuit of beauty and passion alternates with profound boredom. Yet, boredom only intensifies Raysky's eroticism, driving him on from one woman to another. First fascinated by Sofia Belovodov, a cold St. Petersburg society lady, he forgets her for buxom Marfenka, his country cousin, to end up falling hopelessly in love with her darkly attractive sister, Vera, the novel's heroine. Altogether, Raysky has all the cardinal traits of the "superfluous man," by then a somewhat antiquated type, a fact that may account for the elements of parody in Goncharov's portrayal.

Whereas Oblomov returns to his childhood home via dream, Raysky visits his estate, Malinovka. Once more Goncharov uses his favorite device of contrasting two cultures, rural and metropolitan, at the same time showing significant parallels. The St. Petersburg circles in which Raysky moves are stuffy and dull, concealing their dead spirit by heavy folds of decorum and drapery. In presenting this milieu the author uses extensive imagery of death as well as of sleep and confinement: its people lack self-awareness and inner freedom. Sofia, to Raysky, is wrapped in a cocoon, smugly unaware of the world around her and of her own innermost needs. She is a canary in a golden cage, a doll whose old-style marriage—she is a widow—has left her as virginal as ever and seemingly quite contented with her passionless existence. Raysky's ambition is to awaken her from sleep, to bring her out from under the shadow of the family portraits and the ancestral mores they signify. In this part of *The Precipice* the theme of tradition versus novelty is emphatically slanted in favor of the latter. To be sure, Raysky is "not preaching communism" (V, 35) and may seem merely a spineless liberal, but his foil, the prosaic official Ivan Ayanov, is so colorless that, by contrast, he appears admirable.

The transition to the four remaining parts, which take place in a picturesque rural setting, is effected by Raysky's desire to get away from St. Petersburg. Disenchanted both with his futile wooing of Sofia and with his failure as a painter, he gladly accepts his great-aunt's invitation to visit his estate, which she manages for him. This is a real sentimental journey, his first visit since he was a student some fifteen years ago. The pace of the narrative becomes extremely relaxed as, with Raysky as a recording consciousness, the author amplifies the rustic portions already given in Part I with new vignettes of life in the provinces. Besides major figures like Vera and Granny—a petname for Raysky's great-aunt, Tatyana Markovna Berezhkov —there is a host of minor characters: Kozlov, a language teacher at the local high school, and his wife, the vivacious vamp Ulinka; Savely, a dour middle-aged peasant and his chronically unfaithful wife, Marina; and, among the other servants, staid Vasilisa and Yakov, the lady-killer Egor, and gnomelike Ulita. Most of these figures are portrayed with great zest and humor. Even Titus Nikonych Vatutin, Granny's intimate, and Openkin, a somewhat degraded *iurodivyi* (holy fool) who visits regularly once a month, gets drunk on madeira and invariably ends up sleeping it off in the barn—even these figures have a spark of life in them. There are also many incidental characters, such as peasants seen at work, shopkeepers at their counters, and neighboring gentry. Altogether, Goncharov has created a fictional model of an entire rural and small town community.

The first half of *The Precipice* combines two basic novel types: the *Bildungsroman* and the novel of manners—more precisely what the Russians call *bytovoi roman*, the novel of everyday life. But from the moment when, in Chapter 5 of Part III, Raysky finds Vera reading a letter on blue paper, an entirely new element is added. From now on Raysky recedes into the background, while Vera's romance with Mark Volokhov, a young man under police surveillance, becomes the real stuff of the book. First mentioned by Kozlov in a letter to Raysky, Volokhov has by this time been established as a character through several meetings with the latter. He is a sort of nineteenth-century "yippie," a social rebel who rejects every accepted principle and even scorns common decency, to say nothing of the amenities of civilized living. He rarely enters a house the normal way, but prefers to climb in at the window after approaching through the garden. To Raysky he appears as a modern Diogenes, a name that is quite apt; for though Volokhov lacks a barrel, a farm wagon will do, at a pinch, for sleeping quarters. To respectable citizens the young man is a sort of bogey, while sundry teen-agers enthusiastically, though ineptly, respond to his "new truth," a conglomerate of atheism, immoralism and socio-political rebellion—in short, Nihilism. After meeting Vera in the course of his apple-stealing excursions to the Malinovka orchard, Volokhov gains her confidence and affection. Though a sort of beauty and beast combination—Volokhov is associated with various animals—Vera's fascination with him is quite believable, since stodgy, constricting Malinovka offers little in the way of stimulating company.

By the time Raysky turns up, the relationship is quite advanced, though short of physical intimacy. Vera and Volokhov have been seeing each other secretly since the preceding autumn —it is now summer—and the situation is coming to a head. Vera wants to "save" Mark, while he insists that she take him on his terms: no promises. Their favorite trysting place is at the bottom of a steep within the Malinovka park, a place shunned by all except Vera because of its evil reputation. The reason is given in Part I: many years ago a woman and her lover were brutally murdered there by her husband, who then killed himself. The murderer was buried on the site of the crime, which has since reverted to its natural state.

The wattle fence separating the Rayskys' park from the forest had collapsed long ago and disappeared. Trees from the park were mixed with fir trees and with sweetbrier and honeysuckle bushes; intertwining, they formed together an overgrown, wild place, in which was hidden an abandoned half-ruined arbor. (V, 76)

It is in this run-down arbor, situated in a moral no-man's-land, that Mark and Vera have their rendezvous. However, the identity of Vera's lover is withheld until the end of Part III, where it is directly revealed by the author. This causes considerable strain, turning Raysky's continued pursuit of the mystery of the blue letter into tedious and incredible melodrama. The available clues, such as Mark's possession of a rifle and the repeated gunfire with which he summons Vera, could fool no one. It seems to fool Raysky, though; not until Chapter 14 of Part IV, after letting Vera descend to her rendezvous despite his given promise to restrain her, does he resolve the "mystery" by spying on the lovers in their hideaway. This is the night of Vera's "fall," which occurs just after she and Volokhov have decided to part forever.

The rest of the novel, one entire part, is taken up with Vera's rehabilitation. This is a complicated affair involving repeated confessions of her error to intimates, including her admirer Tushin, a bearish landowner-entrepreneur of thirty-eight who proposes to her the day after her downfall. When Mark, willing now to marry her in spite of principle, keeps pestering her with his blue letters, Tushin volunteers to be her messenger. Meanwhile, Granny has assumed a key role in the resolution of Vera's predicament. When, at Vera's insistence, Raysky informs her of the fateful encounter in the arbor, the old lady nearly breaks down. For days she wanders about the estate like a sleepwalker, uttering the ambiguous little phrase *Moi grekh:* "It's my fault" (lit. "My sin"). Only when she discovers that Vera is ill does she recover her former self. Given new hope by Granny's love and understanding, Vera relinquishes her death wish. However, a deeper communion is necessary before she can fully recover, and for this the author reaches back into Granny's past.

The pattern which emerges is one of tragic recurrence, as Vera's impulsive surrender to Volokhov comes to appear as a kind of repetition of Tatyana Markovna's youthful lapse with her friend Vatutin, then her lover, some forty-five years ago. One evening they were caught unawares in the hothouse by Count Sergey Ivanych, a rejected suitor of Tatyana Markovna's. The Count insulted Vatutin, throwing him into an insensate fury checked only by Tatyana's intervention. This is a primitive drama of passion, though quite civilized by comparison with the recalled crime at the bottom of the precipice. Certainly the end result, though cruel, was more civilized: a gentlemen's agreement by which the Count promised not to reveal the incident, while Vatutin agreed never to marry Tatyana Markovna. Vera learns just enough of this story to make her feel that life may still be possible. In the "obligatory scene" the two women, so long estranged because of Vera's stubborn independence, find their way toward a new relationship. This marks

the real turning point for Vera: "the grave turned into a flower
bed" (VI, 345). The only question is, Will she marry Tushin?
Though it is hinted that she will, Goncharov refrains from an
outright "happy" ending. The novel comes to a close with
Raysky's fond memories of Malinovka, especially of Granny,
Marfa and Vera, as he travels in Europe, where he has gone
to take up sculpture.

I The Genesis of the Novel

The Precipice contains a variety of formal elements, some of
which conflict with one another. The chief conflict is between
the Bildungsroman centered on Raysky and the novel-drama
based on Vera and Volokhov, with scenes from everyday life
(bytovoi roman) qualifying both. Apart from being a hero in
his own story, Raysky also provides the point of view through
which the love plot comes to us. Though Goncharov tries to
sustain the quest theme along with the love story, Raysky as
hero comes to seem an encumbrance as, from Part III on, we
get increasingly involved in the Vera-Volokhov romance and
its aftermath.

This conflict goes back to the original intention: to offer
an apology for a "fallen" woman—an idea inspired by rumors
about a connection between Goncharov's widowed mother and
her friend N. N. Tregubov (d. 1849)—along with a study of the
artistic temperament and the plight of the artist in a society
afflicted with Oblomovism. In an instructive examination of the
"creative history" of The Precipice, the Soviet critic O. M.
Chemena stresses the "enormous role" initially attributed to
Granny, by Goncharov himself said to have been partly modelled
on his mother (VIII, 400). The crucial scene of mutual con-
fession in Part V, referred to above as the "obligatory scene,"
was one of the first sketched, though in somewhat different
form and without being connected to a plot. Subsequently,
Vera came to assume the main burden of the apologia.[1] The
importance ascribed to Raysky and the associated socio-psychological theme, also conceived in 1849, is shown by the fact
that when "Sofia Nikolaevna Belovodov" appeared in The Contemporary in 1860 it was offered as a fragment from the un-

finished novel "Episodes in the Life of Raysky." The modest title betrays Goncharov's main difficulty in writing the book, frankly admitted in *Better Late Than Never:* "What caused me most trouble was the architectonics, the reduction of the entire mass of characters and scenes to a shapely whole; and this was one of the reasons for the slowness" (VIII, 80).

The impetus toward a first structuring of his work apparently came from a personal experience, namely, Goncharov's meeting with a number of Decembrist exiles on his return from Japan through Siberia in 1854–55.[2] In the article "Intentions, Problems and Ideas of the Novel *The Precipice*," first published posthumously in 1895, the author states what his original plot idea entailed. Vera falls in love with the outsider—a "more restrained and better educated" person than Volokhov—in disregard of Granny's wishes and of the feelings of the entire community, then marries him and follows him into Siberian exile (VIII, 218). Though this plot is far more liberal in tendency than the one finally adopted, it is difficult to see how it could have unified the author's disparate materials any more effectively. However, one serious flaw of *The Precipice* as we know it would have been avoided: the glaring anachronism of having a Nihilist, allegedly based on observations stemming from 1862 (VIII, 218), appear in a novel which, however vaguely set in time, belongs to pre-Emancipation times in its social and economic background. Incidentally, the author was well aware of this anachronism (VIII, 145).

The rejection of the original plot was due to Goncharov's suspicion that Turgenev had plagiarized it. The plan for *The Precipice* had been confided to Turgenev, apparently in minute detail, in 1855.[3] In July, 1860 Goncharov writes to Sofia Nikitenko:

. . . he took my best passages from me, gems, and played them on his lyre; if he had taken the content it wouldn't have mattered, but he took the details, the sparks of poetry—like the shoots of new life on the ruins of the old, the story of the ancestors, the garden setting, traits of my old lady—it is enough to make one boil. (VIII, 344)

Curiously, he does not mention what may have been the most

painful loss of all—his plot idea. After describing his first plan
in a letter to Catherine Maykov of April, 1869, he notes that
this plot had already been used "a hundred times" (VIII, 398).
Whatever the basis of this assertion, psychologically it is pure
rhetoric: the only competitor who counted to Goncharov was
Turgenev. Most likely, it was the dénouement of *On the Eve*,
Elena's self-exile with the revolutionary Insarov, that caused
him to reject his original plan. As Chemena comments, he could
not tolerate giving the impression of following Turgenev.[4]

According to the Soviet critic, the actual dénouement of the
love plot came to Goncharov only in 1867,[5] several years after
the new image of Vera's lover appeared. This image is a
decidedly debased variant of the earlier figure, befitting the
change from marriage to seduction in the resolution of the
plot.[6] While the originally envisaged character was a liberal, a
"man of the forties" with whom Goncharov could sympathize,
the Nihilist rebel of the 1860's, Volokhov, represents everything
in contemporary life that was anathema to him. Goncharov's
temperament and circumstances were not such as to make him
feel kindly toward the new radicals, whose writings he had
plenty of opportunity to study as a censor; his *bête noire* was
Pisarev, against whom he carried on a sort of vendetta in 1865–
66. While the deteriorating fate of Vera's lover, along with the
more tragic dénouement, is symptomatic of Goncharov's growing
conservatism, it is also a reflection of the intensified ideological
conflict in the 1860's.

Inevitably, the unfavorable reception of *The Precipice* was
to a large degree determined by this latter fact. But there were
also special circumstances. The publication of the novel had
been awaited for so long that nothing but a masterpiece could
have satisfied the expectations of the critics. When, therefore,
it turned out to be seriously flawed, an avalanche of excoriating
reviews streamed from the presses, sufficiently activating Goncharov's latent paranoia to make him write to Sofia Nikitenko
in June, 1869: ". . . I sometimes seriously fear for my reason."[7]
About a year later the effect of the hostile reviews is still apparent in his continued mood of despondency. He tells Sofia
Nikitenko: "I don't do anything, i.e., I do not write, and I
feel that I shall never write again. They have killed me spir-

itually, and they have killed every living talent in me."[8] But despite his complaints of unfair treatment by the reviewers, Goncharov was quite aware of the weaknesses of his work. In early 1869, before the reviews had taken their toll, he humorously compared his novel to a "cumbersome omnibus jogging along a bumpy road" (VIII, 397). And writing to the poet A. A. Fet in August, 1869, in the midst of the critical attacks, he ruefully gives one of the chief reasons for its flaws, its overlong gestation: ". . . *The Precipice* . . . is the child of my heart; I carried it too long . . . in my breast [*pod lozhechkoi*] and so it turned out big and awkward" (VIII, 421).

II *Three Major Themes: 1. Passion, or the Loves of the Parallels*

And yet, with all its flaws—prolixity, longueurs, strained dialogue, gratuitous editorializing, and others—*The Precipice* is a remarkable work of impressive scope. It takes in everything from love to politics, with art, morality, and much else in between. Here we shall focus on three major themes, two of which were discussed elsewhere by the author: passion, humanization, and the "fallen" woman.

The first of these themes permeates Goncharov's fiction. Alexander Aduev yearns for a "mighty" passion, with disastrous consequences, and Oblomov fears its "morbid" promptings. Like George Eliot, who in *The Mill on the Floss* (1860) makes Maggie Tulliver renounce Stephen Guest, Goncharov distrusts passion, seeing it as a destructive force. In his last novel this force threatens to undermine not only religion and morality, but the social order itself. As the setting suggests, Vera and Volokhov conform neither to nature nor to civilization in their sensual orgy in the old arbor. One is reminded of the time-honored myth examined by Denis de Rougemont;[9] for though adultery is practiced only by such "low" characters as Ulinka and Marina, the recurrent imagery of night, illness, and self-destruction betrays the passion archetype. In any case, marriage has an entirely different basis, revealed through the innocent love of Marfa and Vikentiev which counterpoints Vera's hectic romance; their union is one of quiet, tender affection. This represents a "simple, natural" relationship between the sexes, the author says, while all other such relationships in the novel are characterized as "perverted," that is, as marked by "unfortunate or monstrous passions, illnesses which affect the body and soul at once." As causes which induce such illnesses he mentions the presence of obstacles, abuse of love, bad education, and lack of human understanding (VIII, 210).[10]

Despite this harsh judgment, passion is the substance of the book. Goncharov says he had always been aware of the "diverse manifestations of passion" and that, initially carried away by the passion of a "pure and proud" woman, he "involuntarily" came to portray "almost all the forms of passion" in the novel. The "parallels of passion appeared of themselves," he says; they were not due to "algebraic calculation" (VIII, 208–9). Though his hierarchy of feeling, ranging from Tushin's "human" love to Savely's savage craze, is morally based, Goncharov was well aware of the purely esthetic possibilities of the subject; passion, he writes, is conducive to more living characters, "vivid effects and dramatic situations" (209). Moreover, those of his characters who have been in its toils seem to have profited from the experience. Granny's commanding presence is unthinkable apart from her tragic love story, and Vera supposedly becomes more conscious, wise, and humane because of her dark initiation. Compared to them, Marfenka and Vikentiev, said to represent the great majority (97), are simply grown-up children. Inevitably, we are less interested in the model propriety and clean healthy joy of the latter, whether as lovers, engaged couple, or bride and groom, than in those "perverted" passions which the author morally deplores. The pivotal figure in this connection is Raysky, the apostle of passion whose gospel turns sour as the action unfolds.

An artist *manqué*, Raysky fritters away his "excess of imagination" in philandering and facile improvisations. His existence is centered in pure sensation, intensified to agony or ecstasy by an ever active fancy. When in love, he creates an ideal image of the beloved, and it is to this image that he is attached, not the real person. Thus, he loves only "in and with his imagination" (VIII, 214). Accordingly, his concept of passion is quite idealistic. As his name suggests (*rai* means "paradise"), Raysky sees passion as a magic key to the lost paradise. Through it, he seeks both to give meaning to his own life and to arouse others to do the same for themselves. In particular, he wants to awaken Russian women, to whom he dedicates his projected novel, *Vera*.[11] However, Raysky's idealism is belied by certain ironic patterns, and we come to suspect that the real substance of his philosophy, whether it manifests itself as a cult of passion, art or ideal womanhood, is libertinism.

The inner truth of the gospel of passion emerges through a series of distorting mirrors. Besides Volokhov, three women, each engaged upon her own kind of quest, are the chief vehicles of this ironic mirror technique. First, Mme Kritsky, a middle-aged local coquette with mincing airs, overexquisite French and a constant itch for young men, is a parody of Raysky as amorist, in addition to being a caricature of the provincial lion hunter. The satirical intent is evident from the fact that several three-way scenes in which Raysky attempts to "woo" Vera, are spoiled by the intrusion of the importunate double. This is a stock satiric device: causing a character's "humor" or emotional bias to ricochet upon him. Ulinka, Kozlov's lecherous wife, effects a cruder ricochet: on one of his visits she throws a hysterical fit and "rapes" the would-be Don Juan. Her sexual frenzy, a grotesque version of Raysky's ecstasies, exposes the basis of his creed. Both these parallels are sustained by echoes of some of Raysky's pet ideas, such as the ennui of life and the mutual exclusion of love and marriage, in the ladies' small talk. While Ulinka and Mme Kritsky mirror the violence and the false gallantry of passion-love respectively, Marina, the irrepressibly lustful maid, shows up its inbred promiscuity.

The most devastating example of mirroring comes about by way of Volokhov, acting as self-appointed gadfly and sponge to Raysky. Though the two men are far apart in background, manners and social views, they have enough in common to establish a connection. Significantly, they are both associated with the Greek cynic Diogenes, and they are sometimes seen wearing each other's clothes; moreover, Mark spends Raysky's money, which Raysky is too genteel to withhold from him. Both admire Vera and court her assiduously, but neither believes in constant, "eternal" love. What they believe in is sex, Raysky as a transcending experience, Volokhov as the fulfilment of a natural need. The similarities between their eulogies of passion as a rapturous experience conferring true happiness are quite apparent. But while Raysky can only dream of Vera, Volokhov subdues her, thus acting out the other's inmost desire.

The relationship between the two men is reminiscent of that between a person and his double. In its Dostoevskian form, this relationship entails that the morally inferior man acquires a strange power over his semblable, partly depriving him of his moral freedom. Volokhov, a definitely "lower" person than Raysky, manipulates him unconscionably: Raysky seems to be completely powerless against his insolent demands and highly vulnerable to his insults. On the other hand, there are clear hints that Raysky has facilitated Volokhov's designs on Vera. According to her testimony, her cousin's praise of love has made her more susceptible to passion and therefore to Volokhov's influence, a fact that, put bluntly, turns Raysky into a kind of pimp for the cruder man. Though thematically quite different from the Ivan Karamazov-Smerdyakov relationship, the connection between Raysky and Volokhov resembles it in at least one respect: just as Ivan, so to speak, gives the lecture, the justifying arguments, while Smerdyakov carries out the demonstration, so Raysky supplies the sublime love talk while Volokhov performs the seduction. The main difference is that no direct "infection" occurs between the two, Raysky's accessory guilt deriving solely from his demoralizing effect on Vera.

Ultimately, Goncharov relates the harmful psychology of Raysky and Volokhov to a common, quasi-philosophical root, for which we can find no better word than "libertinism." Though Volokhov is philosophically simpler, more one-dimensional, his views are well described by libertinism, which is clearly a part of the Don Juan theme associated with Raysky. It is mainly a matter of degree. The libertinism of Mark is more extreme, militant and consistent, taking in active irreligion as well as free thought and free love. And unlike Raysky's romantic ego cult, Mark's creed finds a formidable opponent in a religiously rooted morality supported by the conservative folkways of the provinces.

2. A Counter-theme: The Making of Man

The second major theme discussed in "Intentions . . . ," that of "the nature of the artist" and its "manifestations in art and life" (VIII, 216), is of lesser interest, partly because it has been treated so much better by others, partly because Raysky is not a real artist, but an esthete and dilettante. Moreover, its social aspect seems both antiquated and unreal, since members of the gentry, despite "lack of artistic education" and the "idle life of almost all of society fifty years ago" (ca. 1826!), nevertheless managed to make an artistic career. The only interesting part of the art theme is the demonstration of what happens when, as in the case of Raysky, the artistic sensibility is projected into life, making of it "now paradise, now a torture." He is either completely identified with his sensations and the objects of his fancy, or he is a victim of cold destructive analysis, traits that may derive from the figures of Don Quixote and Hamlet as interpreted by Turgenev.[12] Raysky, Goncharov comments, is a "person without a distinctive personality, a form which constantly reflects passing phenomena . . . and steeps itself in the color of successive moments" (214). Such a character may be useful as a narrator's proxy, "the wire to which the puppets are attached" (397), but he is intolerable as the major figure in a "three-decker" novel. At this point we shall mention just one idea which Goncharov expresses through him and then develops into one of the major themes of his work.

This is the theme of "humanization" (*ochelovechivaniia*), initially part of Raysky's quest for the perfect woman. Soon after meeting Vera he realizes what a "titanic force" there is in her; but it needs to be "rationally" directed. He conceives of his achievements as her teacher and guide as a "feat of humanization, a duty to which we are all called and without which any progress is unthinkable" (VI, 8).

This idea may be conveniently approached by way of the animal imagery in the book. While often such images are simply part of a burlesque manner, if recurrent they may be significant. Volokhov is a "wolf," Tushin a "bear," and other characters are momentarily associated with different animals. This is crude, but the technique does show some refinements. Thus, at a time when she is in an especially anxious and impassioned state, Vera throughout an entire chapter keeps digging her "thin fingers, like the claws of a bird of prey" (VI, 226), into Raysky's shoulder. This image suggests the precarious nature of civilization, vulnerable to encroachment by the beast in man as soon as his passions are excessively aroused. Gradually, the animal imagery acquires moral overtones, particularly as it affects Volokhov. As the balked immoralist in his last inner monologue ponders what will remain of him in Vera's memory, he can think only of animal traits: ". . . there won't be a trace of man!" (VI, 388). Volokhov transformed into a beast is Goncharov's image of moral anarchy; it is the logical climax to his deployment of animal imagery in *The Precipice*. Despite the obvious tendentiousness of this characterization, negatively it points up the enormous importance of the theme of humanization to Goncharov.

In one form or another this theme pervades Goncharov's fiction. It underlies his critique of an automated or purely instrumental man in *A Common Story* as well as his exposure, through Oblomov's visitors, of the fragmentation caused by success. It also informs Goncharov's quest for an ideal, whether embodied in the fragile nostalgic charm of Lizaveta Aduev or in the prim perfections of Stolz. *The Precipice* also expresses both aspects of this theme. Besides Volokhov's reversion to animalism, paradoxically a result of his one-sided rationalism, there is Raysky's romantic reliance upon the "heart," an attitude which panders to and invites "wolfish" or "tigerish" passion, as in Ulinka's rape (VI, 87). The positive side of the theme emerges through Raysky's changing ideal of woman and through Tushin.

From being simply an erotic object or an embodied *schöne Seele* satisfying the requirements of an idealistic esthetic, woman acquires a religious aura in Raysky's eyes. This corresponds to the general movement of the book, one from esthetic idealism to religious faith. Mediated by suffering, the new attitude frankly recognizes human fallibility and accepts the necessity of constant self-perfection. Only after Vera's "fall" does her name, meaning "faith," assume its full significance, as does that of Granny, the name Berezhkov suggesting "preserver." Directed both against rationalism and romanticism, the new ideal places man firmly within history and a religious tradition.

Vera and Granny reveal the inspiration of the new idea of man; Tushin is its programmatic embodiment. Coming from beyond the Volga and drawing his strength from the Russian hinterland, Tushin is rooted in the tradition of the gentry, enriched with a strong scent of soil and forest. While honoring the amenities characteristic of his class, he also has some of the sturdy qualities of a merchant, such as initiative, industriousness, and practicality. Moreover, in comparing him to a Robert Owen of the Volga, Goncharov stamps him unmistakably as a social progressive, though, unlike Owen, he is neither a socialist nor an atheist. Most likely the author has in mind Tushin's position as *primus inter pares* in relation to his workmen (VI, 395–96). Thus, Goncharov's ideal man is a synthesis of the best traits of three classes, the landed gentry, the mercantile class, and the working class. Psychologically, his make-up is equally balanced, uniting several elements usually conceived as polarities, such as head, heart and soul, conscious and unconscious, theory and practice. A fine blueprint, perhaps, but as we shall see later, one that, like almost any concept of the complete or perfect man, was hard to incarnate believably in artistic form.

3. *The Woman Question*

The third theme mentioned in "Intentions . . . ," that of the "fallen" woman, is more special than the two contrasting themes just discussed; yet the author makes it the focal point of a wide range of contemporary problems. Volokhov disputes convention and authority all along the line and tries in a small way to create discontent among the young. Though Vera is immune to his influence,[13] Goncharov nevertheless uses her predicament as a test case in the struggle between the "new" and the "old truth." For this he has been criticized, on the ground that the seduction lacks ideological significance.[14] Only indirectly, by way of Vera's arrogant disregard of Granny, does a sort of moral battle come about.

Judging from some of his comments, the author saw the key issue as one of self-will: "Vera was drawn into a false position by her independent and proud will. . . . At the end of her drama . . . she finds salvation from despair only in the em-

braces . . . of Granny" (VIII, 218). The chief reason for Part
V of *The Precipice*—in which Vera, crushed by her disaster,
gradually assumes Marfenka's place in relation to Granny—is
precisely to prove this point: the psychic wound incurred in her
skirmish with evil can be cured only by a return to the old
verities. She is redeemed through suffering.[15] This is Goncharov's answer to the arguments about women's emancipation, in
particular Chernyshevsky's novel *What Is To Be Done?* (1863).

With this conservative view clearly implicit in Vera's story,
other statements in "Intentions . . ." may cause some surprise.
Inspired with feminist ardor, Goncharov inveighs against the
double standard in sexual morality and against the cruel treatment of so-called "fallen" women, who are granted no extenu-
ating circumstances and are frequently condemned to continue,
"in hopelessness and despair, . . . along the same path" (VIII,
216). To the fallen woman he opposes the coquette, seen as
someone who, though not fallen in deed, has preserved her
"virtue" only by a fluke, through fear or with a view to advantage, all the while "wasting all feminine feelings on anyone who
comes along . . ." (217). Though admitting that his coquette
in the novel, Mme Kritsky, is a caricature, Goncharov asks point-
blank: Is she not "a hundred times more" a fallen woman than
Vera and Granny, though never guilty "in *deed*"? (219). In
accordance with this slant, he set out to depict in his work "*two
women guilty in deed, but not fallen*" (217), a formula reminiscent of Thomas Hardy's *Tess of the D'Urbervilles* (1891), subtitled "A Pure Woman" in challenge to Victorian hypocrisy.

Goncharov's handling of the theme of the fallen woman has
both good and bad sides. It avoids the worst clichés of senti-
mentalism, the heroine being neither doomed to die nor condemned to eternal spinsterhood. By the same token the resolution
of Vera's story is nontragic; the turbulence of passion is eventually absorbed into the calm stream of life. In view of the novel's
generous admixture of genre scenes, its most realistic element,
the almost happy resolution of Vera's plight is not surprising.
However, one wishes it could have come about without melodrama and without obviously made-up characters.

Melodrama agrees poorly with Goncharov's narrative manner,
yet in *The Precipice* he resorts to it, and quite understandably.

For despite his disclaimer in "Intentions . . ." that the novelist is not a moralist (VIII, 217), in his last novel he even goes further and becomes an ideologue. A novelist concerned with expressing ideas will often choose extreme situations or use an emphatic style. A good example of a situation of this kind is the duel between Bazarov and Pavel Petrovich in *Fathers and Sons*. The extraordinary seduction of Vera in *The Precipice* belongs to the same category, but is less tactfully handled. Essentially, Goncharov exploits this seduction as a pawn in a reckless attack on the new radicalism, and his anti-Nihilist animus tends to drown out not only the enlightened idea of his work but its realistic features as well.

For all her independent ways, Vera reacts to her misfortune precisely like a heroine in a sentimental novel: thinking that life is over, she wishes to die. In the same vein, Tatyana Markovna after forty-five years supposedly feels a profound sense of guilt for her nocturnal escapade in the hothouse. These reactions, along with much else in the characters' behavior, are strained and unbelievable, certainly unrealistic; nor are they the natural accompaniment of an enlightened view of the fallen woman, or of a more humane sexual ethic. On the contrary, they play into the hands of a rigoristic morality, religious obscurantism, and the traditional subjection of women; and this despite Goncharov's creation of Tushin, willing to take Vera for his wife even after her night with Volokhov.

Admittedly, for the position of women to change, men's attitudes toward them must change simultaneously with women's attitudes toward themselves. But Tushin, who could represent a new, more liberal sexual morality, is a cardboard figure. Therefore, marriage to him would be an unreal dénouement, proving nothing.

III   *Character and Theme in* The Precipice

Many critics have commented on Goncharov's extraordinary ability to portray simple characters, whereas he is less successful with more complex and sophisticated ones. V. P. Botkin, in a letter to Fet of June 21, 1869, goes even further. Having characterized *The Precipice* as a "lengthy, verbose rhapsody, wearisome to the point of nausea," he praises the author for his descriptions: "He is more successful at describing things than people."[16] This has a crude ring of truth about it, at any rate enough to highlight some of the strengths and weaknesses of Goncharov's character portrayal in *The Precipice*.

Following those who have praised the Flemish quality of Goncharov's "brush,"[17] we have several times mentioned his talent for genre and indicated the broad representation of everyday life in his works. *The Precipice* has a large proportion of genre scenes and characters, ranging from life in the servants' quarter to festivals and celebrations, from an almost insectlike house serf like Ulita to the fearsome witch doctor Melankholikha and drunken Openkin. Naturally, all of these figures are observed from the outside only, but with a steady eye. More important characters like Marfenka and Vikentiev, also fairly pure expressions of *byt*, are excellently done as long as Goncharov retains his objectivity. However, when he turns the simple, unsophisticated girl into a shining example of the old morality as she tells Granny of her beau's "insolent" proposal, she loses her charm (Pt. III, ch. 16). In another scene she is credited with an impossible dream, one of statues coming alive, solely because Goncharov needs it for his theme of awakening. Both these weak spots are incurred because of poorly handled dialogue, an element of composition that is very sensitive to false touches.

In varying degrees, all the major figures suffer similar damage. Even the colorful image of Granny, often said to be the best-drawn character in the book, is tainted by the author's tendency, his attempt to erect a monument to the "old, conservative Russian life" (VIII, 90). An efficient, domineering and class-conscious lady of the manor whose narrow views are tempered by folk wisdom, Granny is also highly intelligent and possesses a great store of kindness and generosity. The principle which holds this bundle of traits together, as far as her portrayal is successful, is nothing rational, but rather a vigorous zest for life in all its forms and a profound organic sense of her place in the community. The author comes closest to the elemental core of the old lady in an extended animal analogy, by which he evokes her growing suspicion after Vera's misadventure:

. . . from midday on Tatyana Markovna changed so much, scrutinized everybody so suspiciously and listened so attentively to everything, that Raysky compared her to a horse who is carelessly munching his oats, putting his muzzle in up to his ears, and then suddenly hears a rustle or catches the scent of some unknown and invisible enemy. Pricking up his ears and lifting his head, he gracefully turns around and listens motionlessly with wide-open eyes and heavily breathing nostrils. Nothing. Then, slowly, he turns around to his crib and, still listening, unhurriedly shakes his head three times and rhythmically stamps his hoof three times, whether to calm himself, to demand a reason or to warn his enemy of his vigilance—and again he puts his muzzle into the oats; but now he crunches cautiously, lifting his head occasionally and turning around. He is forewarned and has grown wary. He munches, but his shoulder keeps quivering and his ear keeps turning, back and forth and back again. (VI, 299)

A truly epic simile, this passage describes horse and woman at once, without strain. Obviously, to describe a human being directly in such a detailed manner would be demeaning to his dignity, turning him into an object of inspection; on the other hand, a generalization would fall flat. The analogy is the perfect solution: Granny's human dignity is maintained, while at the same time her profound instinctive core of being is evoked.

A comparison of this passage with two longer ones, one in dialogue, the second a kind of lyrical rhapsody, illustrates how art—simplicity, verisimilitude, psychological truth—can be vitiated by a too overt tendency. In the first sequence, following Vikentiev's declaration to Marfenka, Granny goes through the ritual of marital negotiations with the young man's mother, adopting a pose of pompous antiquarianism which is an insult to her intelligence (Pt. III, ch. 18). This is not simply a joke, either on her part or on the author's, but a deliberate plea of respect for the old mores. Deplorably, Goncharov's sense of humor, for which he rightly takes credit in a letter to Sofia Nikitenko in 1860 (VIII, 354–55), in *The Precipice* seems curiously impaired. While Oblomov is treated with the equilibrium of a mind which can contain irreconcilables and live with uncertainties, allowing the character to acquire depth and body, in Goncharov's last novel we sometimes get only a profile, or a series of contradictory profiles, of the characters. One such profile of

Tatyana Markovna is the heavy-handed cliché of the "fallen ruler," repeated *ad nauseam* in the lyrical rhapsody just referred to (Pt. V, ch. 7). In this passage, while Granny is wandering about the fields in despair because of Vera's misfortune, Raysky perceives her grief and her grandeur through images of great women in history. The meretriciousness of the author's poetic prose momentarily turns a living woman into a relic.

Other characters fare worse, for different reasons. Both Tushin and Mark Volokhov, good and bad guy respectively, are schematic, Tushin more so. First, he is introduced too late and dropped for too long, considering his important role as the answer to Volokhov; that is, he is too minor to assume the burden of that role. Secondly, he is too thematically conceived and too abstractly presented; the author himself admitted he was "contrived" (VIII, 423). In his behavior he is directed by his creator, who holds him strictly to his script. The resulting puppet quality is particularly apparent in his meeting with Volokhov on the site of the old arbor. In this scene he speaks to Volokhov as if reading from a book of etiquette; indeed, one has the impression that it is Goncharov the connoisseur of the amenities who represents Vera at the rendezvous.[18] Still, there is something real in Tushin, as shown by his social awkwardness, his love of bear-hunting and, especially, his periodic drunken sprees with his cronies. There is nothing comparable to this emotional generosity in Stolz. Nevertheless, like Stolz, Tushin must buckle under to Goncharov's grand design and be an ideal human being, as well as a perfect gentleman. In the process of making him so, Goncharov spoils his best effects and the poetry is lost in the program.

Critics have objected to Mark Volokhov as a caricature, and they are right. Though Goncharov used the same extreme device of characterization in creating Oblomov, a sort of human slug, in his case the all but grotesque exaggeration discloses a complex, idiosyncratic inner life. Georg Lukács says that "by this 'exaggeration' all the mental conflicts engendered by Oblomov's sloth are thrown into bold relief. . . ."[19] But in Mark's case the human complexity is lacking; he is little more than an emblematic symbol of the author's contempt and hatred for the so-called "new men."

Only in his early meetings with Raysky, and in sporadic glimpses here and there, does Volokhov appear as a living character. He is not only intelligent but also sensitive, and a shrewd judge of people. His opinion of Raysky cuts through the bland hypocrisies and self-deceptions of polite society. Stripping the veils of idealization from Raysky's cult of beauty, he exposes the underlying cause, eroticism, and with a cynic's privileged vision sums him up as a "dud" (*neudachnik*). Some of these traits are undoubtedly a residue of the initial Mark, a Bohemian radical of the 1840's related to the "Byronists" of the preceding generation.[20] If this image were sustained and deepened, as by the "autobiography" of Mark which Goncharov wrote but did not include,[21] his bizarre behavior would acquire the human content it so sorely needs, as that of Lermontov's hero, Pechorin, does through the more psychological portions of "Princess Mary" (in *A Hero of Our Time*).

With the "new man" of the 1860's superimposed upon the earlier figure, a process of which Goncharov was perfectly aware (VIII, 401), the burlesque style of portrayal becomes out of place. For while such a hyperbolic style can successfully convey a social attitude, it can only make a travesty of an entire philosophy, however crude. Being concrete and vivid, Mark's exaggerated features—his habit of entering a house by the window, his mutilations of books, his sponging on Raysky, his sleeping in a wagon—memorably evoke his supreme contempt of society; generally, his devil-may-care attitude and hobo manners are the best part of his portrayal. But the attempt to connect these traits with the philosophy of Nihilism is a failure: his bizarre actions remain mere eccentricities without ideological importance. And where the author tries to convey his "philosophy" and moral substance directly, the character gets swallowed up in the doctrine.

In the dialectical haze enveloping the scenes between Vera and Volokhov, Goncharov seems to lose all sense of the reality of his characters. Their meetings are virtual debates in which naturalistic philosophy confronts a religious concept of man. In one way or another, both characters become vehicles of the author's *Weltanschauung*, Volokhov in the process losing his good judgment and keen psychological sense, along with his residual humanity. However, worse is yet to come. After his encounter with Tushin, Mark is given an internal monologue—a technique for which Goncharov had no particular flair—in which he expresses his reaction to the collapse of his affair. The result is a monologue-sermon in which the author violates the integrity of his own character: he breaks into its inmost recesses and, clearing out the furniture, uses the empty walls as a resonance chamber for his own views. Though he does the same with Raysky, in his case the treatment is excessively flattering, so that at the end the "dud" becomes almost a positive hero. But, really, is there such a great difference between Mark and Raysky? A cynic might say: Raysky is nothing but Mark with *Kinderstube*. But while one is condemned, the other undergoes apotheosis.

Vera, Goncharov's darling—he says she was his ideal at the time she was conceived (VIII, 400)[22]—suffers as a character because, in direct contrast to Volokhov, she is too close to his old man's heart. At first presented as a saucy provincial beauty, she delights the reader by the way she puts down Raysky, who richly deserves her scorn by his adolescent importunities. Apart from being intriguing, her secretive ways bespeak a free spirit, a welcome relief in the midst of so much provincial mediocrity. Though she is never seen with a book, she is evidently a well-read person familiar with advanced thought in many fields. And yet, this intelligent, knowledgeable young lady falls victim to a devouring passion, for which she blames Raysky and his libertine preaching. Goncharov must have it both ways: Vera, to be meaningful as a symbol of the best in Russian womanhood, must be intelligent and well-read; however, for her "fall" to be possible she must also be vulnerable to vehement passion: a pretty neat trick, something like grafting a gypsy onto a bluestocking. This is no trivial matter, because Vera's passionate nature is the direct occasion for the religious turn in her life, by which Granny's "old truth" triumphs over Volokhov's "new lie." Initially she is seemingly indifferent to religion, but suddenly one day Raysky finds her praying in the chapel (Pt. III, ch. 15). From that point on a continuous tug-of-war is supposedly taking place within her between those forces which pull her down the precipice to Mark and those which draw her to the chapel and

Granny: she becomes a sort of victim of the generation gap.

However, this inner battle is not very convincing. Rather, there seem to be two Veras, one a secular devotee of freedom, the other a follower of orthodox religion and traditional morality; which is the more real is a matter of taste. To us it looks as if the seeds of a truly independent, self-reliant Vera were squashed by fiat of the author, fearful of following out the inner logic of his initial conception. And so we are left with a quite ordinary girl whose rebellious phase may be dismissed, along with her Gothic preference for the gloomy old house, as a romantic whim without deeper significance. In any case, she soon forgets Volokhov, being wounded in her pride rather than her heart. The effect of her reading, quite exaggerated, seems equally superficial; apparently it was never assimilated. The implied contradiction between the authorial voice and Vera's nature as shown by her behavior indicates Goncharov's loss of critical focus in regard to his character. Perhaps he shared some of the uncertainty of Raysky, his alias, who vacillates from one extreme to another in his view of Vera. When she annoys him he sees her as an average girl from the sticks, but as soon as she makes a friendly gesture he raises her to symbolic status. However, instead of exalting her, Raysky's shoddy lyricism has a banal effect.

A pattern begins to emerge in Goncharov's character portrayal in *The Precipice*. The first half of the novel, though lacking drama and a great theme, is fairly realistic, dominated by the epic calm we associate with Goncharov; the last two parts, those in which Vera's fall and redemption take place, are in spots so contrived as seriously to damage the entire novel, though the author thought they were the best (VIII, 111). One reason for this decline is evident from the portrayal of Vera and Volokhov: the characters are somehow changed, not through experience, but because of a shift in authorial tendency. Raysky, the central figure, suffers most of all from this kind of manipulation. For the Don Juan who encourages Mme Belovodov to break out of her prison[23] is the diametrical opposite, or nearly so, of the man who watches the end of Vera's drama. From being a person who loves to *épater le bourgeois* and to awaken young women to a new awareness of self and society, he becomes a celebrant of the status quo; the iconoclast turns into a kind of idol worshiper, bowing down before images of past greatness.

The very conception of a character sometimes precludes change. In Raysky's case, fundamental change contradicts the pattern he follows in the book, flitting from one woman and vocation to another, from city to country and back again, finally to leave for Europe to pursue his latest mirage. Basically, he is a comic figure, with some features of the picaresque hero. Apart from this, the unconscious process of moral growth that Raysky supposedly undergoes has to be taken on faith; it is not dramatized.

With beating heart and a thrill of pure tears he overheard, amid the filth and noise of passion, a quiet subterranean work going on in his human essence, some sort of mysterious spirit . . . calling him . . . to hard, neverending work on himself, on his own statue, on the ideal of man.

The ponderous language alone is enough to make one skeptical of this "subterranean" activity. Apparently, something like sublimation is intended, because the author continues:

Due to this consciousness of creative work within himself, the passionate, caustic Vera now disappeared from his memory, and if she turned up again it was only because he summoned her, with a prayer, to the work of the mysterious spirit, in order to show her the sacred fire within himself and to kindle it in her. . . . (VI, 207)

Regrettably, the only tangible evidence of change shows that it has been for the worse, as Raysky increasingly becomes a vehicle of inflated lyrical passages, whether to celebrate the new beauty of Granny and Vera, or the destiny of Russian women in general. What a relief under these circumstances to discover that Goncharov is still capable of the light touch, as in the last scene between Raysky and Mme Kritsky, in which the lady tries to wangle out the truth behind the spicy rumor about Granny (Pt. V, ch. 21). Instead of giving us a rhapsody or a sermon, the author simply reveals a humorist's frank delight in the vagaries of human nature.

Though the relationship between character and theme in *The Precipice* is a complex one, one generalization may be offered.

Whereas in *Oblomov* the theme, broad and all-encompassing, mostly grows out of the characters and therefore an illusion of reality is sustained, in *The Precipice* all too frequently the themes interfere with truth, falsifying the psychology of the characters and turning elements of composition like dialogue, internal monologue, and *erlebte Rede* into vehicles of authorial rhetoric. A similar process of constraining the real is evident in Goncharov's handling of symbolic imagery.

IV *Imagery and Symbolism in* The Precipice

Goncharov told the truth when, in a letter to Sofia Nikitenko, he said there was "much poetry" in him (VIII, 363); it is also part of his work. His last novel, like *Oblomov*, shows clear signs of being a "poetic" novel. However, unlike its predecessor *The Precipice* is lyrically conceived; that is, it is conceived as a species of self-expression and is held together by a scheme of imagery and symbol which arises from this conception. In recent times *Doctor Zhivago* is the best example of this kind of novel, a great poet's novel. But whether written by a great or a minor poet, such a novel tends to have certain distinctive qualities: historical reality is freely handled, characters tend to be symbols of the author's values, and symbolic motifs form a basic element of structure. We need not consider all of these traits, of which the first is implicit in Goncharov's casual acceptance of anachronism, while the second is sufficiently evident from our discussion of theme and character. But the third is well worth examining.

Of the many image patterns in *The Precipice*, one of the most apparent is the opposition between flow and fixity, usually expressed through water and stone imagery. Water, an archetypal life symbol, is associated with the workings of the imagination, with art as experience. The following passage conveys Raysky's impressions as he hears a neighbor play the cello: "The sounds obediently wept and laughed, seemed to bathe him in a wave of the sea, cast him into the deep and then suddenly threw him upon the heights and carried him into airy space." He listened "with a tremor of near terror to these wide-flowing waves of harmony" (V, 112). Art through Goncharov's imagery acquires a space of its own, where ordinary laws of motion no longer hold

and where forms dissolve into swirling undulations. This world
of the imagination is continuous with memory, whose emotive
depths are stirred by Raysky's listening to his schoolmate Vasyu-
kov's playing. "The figure of a woman [his mother] revived more
and more clearly in his memory, as if in these moments she had
risen from the grave to appear as alive" (V, 57). One is reminded of a *Künstlernovelle* like Thomas Mann's *Tonio Kröger*
(1903), in which images of life and home such as sea, walnut
tree, and fountain are grouped with the art motif, the violin.

The opposing image, the statue, is applied mostly to the
"pillars" of society, petrified or ossified forms of life which require the breath of an artist to come alive. Consequently,
Raysky's dream is to become a sort of Pygmalion, one who will
rouse dead, inert Russia, especially its women, from stony sleep.
At the end of Part I Raysky has a vision in which he sees a
woman in stone in the rocky desert, yearning for awakening.
Suddenly there flashes a "bright light, the leaves trembled on
the trees and streams of water began to purl. . . ." Then, among
a swirling play of light and color, "a wave of life ran along her
thighs" and the statue comes to life (V, 154–55). Apart from
several minor repetitions, Marfenka's dream of how the statues
in the Count's gallery came alive is an elaborate restatement of
the Pygmalion theme (VI, 161–62). This sculptural conceit is,
as it were, embodied in the action of the novel when, driven by
her agony of grief, Granny leaves her house to wander around
the estate: it was "as if a bronze monument had stepped down
from its pedestal and started moving . . ." (VI, 322).

Through this imagery, mostly projected through Raysky and
at the end psychologically explained by his newly discovered
talent for sculpture, Goncharov also seems to convey another
idea, that of moral perfection. Thus, Vera "was forming for
herself a strong, living life out of the old 'dead' life—and to him
[Volokhov] as to Raysky she was a sort of beautiful statue,
breathing with original life, living by her own mind, not a
borrowed one, and by her own proud will" (VI, 270). Both
spiritual torpor and moral perfection are understandable as
symbolic meanings of "statue," but confusion arises when they
appear together in the same work. Eventually, it is true, the
"deadness" initially connoted by the word "statue," as by the

ancestral portraits, seems largely forgotten; all the same the ambiguity is never resolved and seriously flaws the novel's symbolic scheme.

Other images enter more naturally into the texture of the work, like those which arise from the landscape with its fauna and flora, and atmospheric ones like clouds, thunderstorms and lightning. Some of them, like birds, are also associated with interiors. Through frequent figurative use, the bird images come to express definite socio-moral and philosophical concepts. Raysky likes to speak of caged birds, an epithet he applies both to Sofia and Marfenka. Other phrases have reference to the notion of a "nest of the gentry," used as the title of a Turgenev novel and connoting an entire way of life. Marfenka likes to stay around the "nest," Vera does not. But there are all sorts of birds, predatory ones, for example, or "nocturnal" birds like Volokhov. In connection with the theme of passion we have commented on the crude naturalism expressed through such images. Volokhov, who likes to speak in terms of bird imagery, believes in imitating "Nature, red in tooth and claw," but the fledgling from the nest of Malinovka finds his philosophy unattractive. Goncharov rings similar changes on his other animal images. Though respectable enough, this bird and beast talk falsifies the dialogue by the language of fable, as in the long debate between Vera and Volokhov (Pt. IV, ch. 1), and overloads the author's narrative with too many coded symbols.

Any writer using a rustic setting will exploit the weather and the changing seasons to create atmosphere and pace the story. Appropriately enough, Vera's seduction occurs in late September and is followed by cloudy days and descriptions of a dying season. This is simply sympathetic coloring, or lyrical use of setting. But as in *Oblomov*, though less successfully, Goncharov goes further, so that gradually the sense of an inner landscape and a weather of the soul suggests itself.

To illustrate by just one example: a thunderstorm in Part III, however vividly described in itself, is most important for its contribution to character portrayal and to Goncharov's symbolic scheme. Vera is fearless, Granny and Marfenka are scared. Granny prays during the storm and asks the others to do the same; Marfenka goes to bed and buries her head under the

pillows. However, this mildly humorous way of suggesting different attitudes soon gives way to more weighty matters. Granny
says something about "thunderstorms" happening in life too,
which makes it important to have a good man on the box—an
allusion to Tushin who has just accomplished a ticklish maneuver
up the steep (*obryv*) with his carriage. The "symbolic" idea
here disclosed not only underlies the frequent occurrence of
words like "thunder," "thunderstorm," "stormcloud," and "lightning" in the parts about Vera, but also suggests the future role
of Tushin in her life.

Such a symbolic style can be very effective if used tactfully,
permitting a muted indirect expression which at the same time
is concrete and immediate. However, if it becomes compulsive
and didactic, the effect soon wears off and one is left only with
rhetoric. This is even more so with traditional images like "fire"
and "light" discussed in connection with *Oblomov*. "Fire" mostly
functions in its destructive aspect in Goncharov, and in *The
Precipice* there is a scorching amount of it. One is reminded of
Hawthorne, whose symbolic technique is similar, though far
more economical. At its worst, the pseudo-imagist style of the
novel tends both to confuse and inflate language: words no
longer have their ordinary meanings and the insistent use of
metaphor precludes simplicity and directness. A smile always
"flashes," passion invariably "burns," and a frown "darkens" the
brow. Instead of disclosing the real, such heavy, hackneyed
"imagistic" rhetoric conceals it under vaguely conceived archetypes.

The most important symbol in the book is the one in the title,
and this is handled quite well. The word used simply means
"steep," a precipitous slope, but in the text this word is richly
supplemented by others such as *propast'* (gulf) and *bezdna*
(abyss), with both literal and figurative meanings. As a result
of the combined use of these related words, the bottom of the
precipice where much of the action takes place becomes a sort
of bottomless pit, connoting irreligion, immorality, social rebellion, and catastrophe—indeed, everything which threatens the
established order and the Christian faith. Conversely, imagery
of heights is related to positive values. In his contemplated
dedication to his novel within the novel, Raysky refers to having

called the women of Russia up to the mountain to work toward the perfection of their souls (VI, 420). More centrally, Vera, who "falls" from the heights down the precipice, is retrieved from the pit by Granny and Tushin; the latter says he will throw a bridge across the precipice and carry Vera to safety. Basically, this is an emblematic presentation of the Christian pattern of fall and redemption. Other features reinforce this pattern. Volokhov is a tempter, a sort of devil figure, and the passion through which he lures his Eve to ruin is enveloped in "serpent" imagery; Volokhov even mimics the Biblical serpent, saying that with the new freedom they shall be "like gods" (VI, 318). Goncharov, then, is writing a reenactment of the fall of man, giving the drama a broad social and cultural orchestration.

Most obvious are the religious and the social analogues of Vera's personal drama. Volokhov, the outcast, is the representative of a crude force for change in Russian life, a force that puts itself against the established order on all fronts. As an atheist he is the "wolf" that breaks into the fold of believers, attacking "faith" (*vera*) itself. The wolf is cast out once more and faith is victorious. Socially, the rootless Volokhov, possibly of nongentry background, represents rebellion from below, Tushin being anxious that he might dare to ascend the steep (VI, 373). But no accommodation is contemplated with the "new force": Volokhov's proposal of marriage is rejected both by Vera and Granny. The reconciler is Tushin, a gentleman who at the same time is said to embody a new progressive force, the real "party of action" in Raysky's words (394).

The Greek myth of Demeter and Kore may underlie certain symbolic usages that go beyond the Christian archetype of redemption, while being in accord with it. This myth, symbolizing an eternal struggle between the forces of darkness and destruction and those of preservation and light, is suggested in particular by the relationship between Vera and Granny, referred to several times as mother and daughter. Though no direct allusions are made to these mythological figures in the novel, there are several to Isis, identified by the Greeks with Demeter.[24] In her capacity as a thrifty manager of Malinovka, Granny is a worthy incarnation of Demeter, Earth Mother and

goddess of agriculture; several times called the ruler of a kingdom, at the very end Granny is seen by Raysky as Mother
Russia herself. Through his reenactment of Demeter's wander-
ings in search of her lost daughter, abducted by Hades, the
author betrays a distinctly feminine religious sensibility. This
sensibility is tuned to the sacred mystery of life itself, as shown
by the context of the author's allusions to Isis, consistently associated with the idea of a mysterious secret which modern science
is working to dispel.[25] Judging by the action of the champion
of scientism in the novel, Volokhov, its effect is indeed destructive, causing the realm of Granny-Demeter to be thrown into
temporary disarray.

Though myth may be effective in ordering a complex series of
events, it usually tends to oversimplify these events, making
them conform to universal patterns. Insofar as it uses symbolic
myth, whether Christian or Greek, The Precipice does not offer
an objective portrayal of social reality; instead it presents a
highly personal vision.

V Concluding Evaluation of The Precipice

The variety of symbolic imagery in The Precipice, artistic,
natural and mythic, considerably qualifies the novel's realism.
Evidently, Goncharov wanted above all to convey a Weltanschauung, the fruit of his experience both as man and artist.
This is confirmed by a letter of 1868 in which he says: "In this
work are transposed into images my own convictions, rules and
impressions, and all this is drawn from the good, healthy and—
I dare say—honest sources of life."[26] As this statement implies, his
vision was to be an affirmative one, a factor which goes far to
explain the book's weaknesses.

Traditionally, Russian writers of Goncharov's generation failed
when the critical attitude (otritsanie) was replaced by a positive
tendency. An exposé can never dispense with realism, even when
it takes the form of allegory, while didacticism often does.
Goncharov's desire to communicate a "message" to his contemporaries turns the history of his last novel into a tragic
repetition of Gogol's failure in the continuation of Dead Souls,

with the difference that his project was completed. A mediocre thinker and a rather narrow moralist, Goncharov falls short of his stature as a supreme artist when encroaching upon alien territory. The sense of his own characters leaves him as he develops lengthy arguments obviously unfit for them, strains their dialogue with obtrusive motifs or elevates them to symbolic status.

Symbolic writing which violates the real is usually either confused or it becomes allegory; Goncharov's practice has a touch of both. But while the confusion is part of a general structural defect, his tendency towards allegory stems from his inability successfully to join the One and the Many, the rich variety of experience with the idea. The two realms tend to break apart, creating not a comic but a distressing incongruity. In this respect, it is instructive to observe the extreme outer limit to which Goncharov will carry allegory. By the very end the author in pseudo-classical style introduces a triad of personified abstractions, Nature, Art and History, which are said to accompany Raysky on his travels in Europe. Since they appear in close conjunction with his three beloved women, Marfenka, Vera and Granny, one wonders whether these are not, at least momentarily, conceived as the human embodiments of those abstractions. But apart from this extreme example, more general evidences of allegory exist in the triteness and the rather mechanical handling of some of the symbols, as well as the authorial constraint exerted upon the characters. Of course, Goncharov's shortcomings were not unique, and in view of the fact that symbolic fiction at the time had neither an esthetic nor a tradition, they were all but unavoidable.

The cardinal fault of *The Precipice* is a structural one: it has a broken back. In addition to the change in focus occurring in Part III, there is another in tendency, and a third in style. The shift in narrative focus makes Raysky superfluous except as an observer, but all the same the reader must endure long arid stretches of his banal, involuted self-reflections. The change in tendency is evident in many ways, some implicitly discussed in connection with the character portrayal. While splitting the characters, it also adversely affects the symbolic scheme. For example, the Pygmalion-Galatea conceit is a pervasive motif; as we have shown, it is even acted out. Yet, it does not really inform the book as a whole: no statues come alive. Mme Belovodov merely makes a silly *faux pas* with Milari,[27] while Granny, despite her act of contrition, ends up on a higher pedestal than ever.

Equally damaging is the change in Goncharov's language, anticipated already in Raysky's first meditations on Vera. However, in the last two parts the rhetoric becomes quite unconstrained; it is as if the author's youthful romanticism is breaking through the barrier of repression. At the same time the behavior of the characters, in Part V continuously in tears or sharing sexual secrets, becomes more tainted with melodrama and sentimentality. Phrases like "quivering passion," "evil brilliance," beauty "sparkling like the night" or enveloped in a "mysterious veil," suggest the high-pitched tone of the narrative, as if style has to do for substance. Worst are the long-winded analytical and expository passages, which betray a lack of talent to *dramatize*. This makes the novel unduly drawn out. Goncharov would have been wiser to omit the commentary, but then, of course, his precious "message" might be jeopardized.

What that message is, however, one hardly knows; language and thought cannot be separated. His thinking is worth attending to only when it is implicit, absorbed within the shapes and rhythms of his created world. When he waxes "profound," his thought becomes banal and his language trite and pretentious. Occasionally, Goncharov's writing sounds like a prose ode in the style of Lomonosov. His aspiration to monumentality is the more deplorable as even in old age Goncharov was capable of racy narrative, to judge by the "Fish Soup" (*Ukha*), a delightful farce from his latest years.[28]

The Precipice is a frustrating book. Vaguely conceived, on a grand scale, it was elaborated through years of mental anguish and delivered in pain. All too clearly it shows the struggle of the author to shape his inner world, torn by many conflicts—between old and new, art and life, intellectual freedom and traditional constraints, between the nostalgia of youthful memories and the cruel urgencies of contemporary history. His artistic problems are reflected in Raysky, who periodically enters in his notebook as material for a novel what Goncharov has already given us as the finished product. This device is not quite what the Russian formalists call "exposure of the method" (*obnazhenie priëma*), used by such writers as Pirandello, Gide, Aldous Huxley, and others, though if brought to a significant point it might have become that. Raysky's attempt to write is not exploited as a source of yet another perspective on life. Rather, his role as a would-be writer annoyingly interferes with the illusion of reality, without any evident compensation. What are we to think of a character who not only makes, and records, the same observations of life as the author has already presented, but until the very end means to shape a novel from them? The relationship between the author and Raysky is quite confusing. Having made a belated embodiment of his youthful romantic self,[29] Goncharov seems to view his character as belonging to the same ontological order as himself, since what the one cannot shape, the other (Goncharov) simply publishes. Is the author ridiculing Raysky, who goes to sleep à la Oblomov over his novel, or is he laughing at himself, admitting the reader to his creative laboratory and using Raysky to reflect his own agonizing struggle with his material? The fact that such questions come to mind means there is something fundamentally wrong with the way the artist-hero functions in the book.

In its confusion of tendencies, novel forms, styles, and artistic techniques, *The Precipice* belongs to no style and is too amorphous to fit any particular novel type. It transcends all categories —but, unfortunately, not because it is a unique masterpiece but because it is a unique failure. Goncharov obviously felt hampered writing in the realistic tradition; he was groping for something new. The lyrical conception, the contrapuntal movements of the characters, the structural role of symbolic motifs, the use of a recording consciousness and of a novelist *manqué* writing a novel within the novel—these are all features more readily found in twentieth- than in nineteenth-century fiction. Apparently, the author did not fully grasp the implications of what he was doing; had he done so he would hardly have ventured to apply all these relatively untried devices in a work of such magnitude. And into this chaos of literary materials, untested techniques and styles falls the ingredient that is to shape it all—his tendency, a disenchanted and disturbed man's attempt to create a firmly established world. No wonder that the baby, to pick up his own metaphor, got "big and awkward." But readers have found the book continuously interesting despite its deformities. A museum piece, yes, but what an extraordinary one, possessing more life than several "living" novels of a minor order.

CHAPTER 6

The Art of Goncharov

IN reviewing *A Common Story* and Herzen's *Who Is To Blame*, Belinsky distinguished between two kinds of writers, the conscious thinker and the "poet-artist."[1] Using slightly different terms, "conscious" and "unconscious" creation, Goncharov agrees with Belinsky that he belongs to the critic's second category and repeats the latter's remark that he was above all carried away "by his ability to draw." He continues:

As I draw, I seldom know at the moment what my image, portrait, or character means: I only see him alive before me—and watch whether I draw correctly. I see him in action with others and therefore I see scenes and draw the others, sometimes far ahead of the novel's plan, not yet quite foreseeing how all the parts of the whole that, by now, are scattered about in my head are to be connected. (VIII, 70)

It is worth noting that the preconceived plan does not direct the working of his imagination. On the contrary, the latter is completely independent, to the point of assuming a hallucinatory presence, and the process of writing acquires an automatic quality. Writing to Lkhovsky after the creative miracle of Marienbad in 1857, he says that

much appeared unintentionally; somebody sat invisibly beside me and told me what to write. For example, in my plan a woman was noted down as passionate, but the pencil made the first stroke quite differently and went on to complete the drawing according to this stroke, and another figure came out. (VIII, 291)

As E. A. Lyatsky comments, his talent mastered the writer rather than vice versa.[2]

However, Goncharov's emphasis on unconscious creation, his assumption that reality was reflected in his imagination as in a mirror, "apart from my consciousness" (VIII, 72), is somewhat exaggerated; besides, other statements conflict with it. His creative process was considerably more complex. One critic distinguishes between three stages: 1) unconscious vision, 2) reflection and testing (*poverka*) and 3) structuring (*arkhitektonika*).[3] The last stage was the most difficult, to judge by a letter of 1860 where Goncharov says: "It is not difficult to draw, at least not for me . . . ; but to develop the meaning, determine the aim of the work, the *necessity* by which the whole work must be sustained—this is both boring and inexpressibly difficult" (341). In *Better Late Than Never* he says that "the structuring alone . . . is enough to absorb the entire intellectual activity of the author"; he mentions, among other things, the handling of the action, the characters' roles and their mutual relations. While the writer's "instinct" helps in the execution of the design, "the mind lays down . . . the main lines, the situations, and devises the necessities . . ." (112). The dichotomy apparent in these statements between his talent, intuitive and organic—he speaks of how his work "grew" and "matured" in him (113)—and his thought, is more or less evident in everything that he produced. While he wrote from inspiration, he tended to order what was given him according to a deliberate scheme.

I Goncharov's Artistic Method

Our discussion has implicitly shown the dual nature of Goncharov's art, with its masterly rendering of the variety of experience on the one hand and the construction of intellectual schemata on the other. Goncharov had an unfailing eye for the contours of the physical world and was an excellent mimic—in the sense, that is, of reproducing the external movements of life. His genre pictures catch the tone and tenor of everyday life with great verve and delicate precision. One critic connects this gift with his "centripetal" sense,[4] which attuned him to village life, local color, and folklore. Within this domain his art assumes the appearance of a spirited improvisation, with only minimal concern for the esthetic effect; the author simply revels in the plenitude of life. At the other extreme is the carefully arranged sequence, whether landscapes, portraits or dialogues, all held together by a dominant idea. The best of Goncharov fuses the idea and the real in a concrete universal.

While "Ivan Savich Podzhabrin" and *The Frigate "Pallada"* offer the purest examples of genre sketches, his first novel, *A Common Story*, is rigorously controlled by an idea. Its portraits are simple, with little light and shadow, and its landscapes are done in strict monochrome. The description of Peter Aduev gives a mere outline: we know how he is regarded by members of his social circle, but his manners, designed to hide his feelings, preclude anything individual. He is a pure type. Alexander's initial "portrait" sets up a contrast between the country bumpkin he once was and the city man he has become, making him representative of a stage of life and a common social situation. Julia is an exemplification of "weak nerves" and a bad education. Nadenka's portrait, too, embodies only one trait, changeability, shown successively in her face, movements, and speech. Much of the dialogue illustrates these traits, or it is held together by specific themes. Similarly, the night on the Neva, one of the novel's few landscapes, adheres strictly to one dominant impression, stillness; an idyl, it marks the romance it envelops as an escape from life. Later, in *Oblomov*, this one-dimensional method is in abeyance; Stolz alone—a man "all bone, muscle and nerve" (IV, 167)—is flat, an expression of the "golden mean." In *The Precipice* Volokhov's traits are unified by their antisocial coloring, Tushin is a tower of strength—*tusha* means a "hulk of a man"—and the essence of Raysky is defined by the opening descriptive trait: a lively, changeable physiognomy. Even Vera, with her "double" look, is described in conformity with an idea, namely, that of the precipice from which she will fall: she has a "bottomless" gaze, her glance draws one into the "depths."

These patterns demonstrate a deep concern with the clarity and unity of the artistic effect. One senses the discipline of a classical taste behind this practice, as contrasted with the baroque portrayals of a Gogol; for though unified by one basic trait, the latter are abundantly rich and varied. In his first and, to a lesser degree, his last novel, Goncharov seems to hold back his "instinct" to draw. But in *Oblomov* he creates artistic pat-

terns in landscape, character portrayal and dialogue that are far
more spontaneous.

Here even burlesque characters and scenes—whether Tarantiev
with his loud empty talk or Zakhar with his whiskers and his
torn coat—acquire a depth of intense life. While Oblomov's
gentlemen visitors are pale stereotypes from a book of etiquette
and Alexeyev and Mukhoyarov are no less flat, Tarantiev's
"humor," his windbag quality, is amplified by an assortment of
traits that relate him to Oblomov. He, too, is a victim of his
background, a do-nothing with a "dormant" power within him
(IV, 42). However, besides representing one variety of Oblomovism, he is also an individual. Unlike Julia in *A Common Story*,
a straight example of bad education, he has a pulsating life of
his own. The same may be said of Zakhar. It is true that the
author's elaborate description of Zakhar, with his slovenliness,
clumsiness and petty thievery, is held together by the valet's
incongruous position between two ages, so to speak; but Zakhar's
distinctive contribution to the novel's theme does not deprive
him of psychological depth. Significantly, both these figures are
endemic to the Russian national scene, for which Goncharov had
a prodigious flair. The most splendid example of this gift,
"Oblomov's Dream," unites vivid realism with a deliberate
theme: the idea and the real attains a perfect fusion.

At the highest level the synthesis achieved by Goncharov
between sensory immediacy and the underlying idea, between
material and structure, is truly admirable. A great deal depends
upon the skill with which motifs are used, mostly in the form
of physical details; some of these have been examined, especially those that have structural and thematic significance. As
long as they are used tactfully so as not to violate the changing
contours of reality, they effectively fulfil their double function:
to evoke a concrete image and convey a unifying concept. The
same applies to the character motifs, in the use of which Goncharov anticipated Tolstoy, just as he developed the "language
of gesture" which tells the true story.

Character motifs define and suggest at the same time; while
implying identity, they also render the movement of life and
take on new colors as the action proceeds. The portrayal of
Olga, allegedly a "model of harmony and grace" and "artisti-

cally formed," comes alive only when the author describes her face, referring to the "light" of thought in her eyes, her thin compressed lips, and the "tiny wrinkle" over one eyebrow. These motifs, especially the eyebrows, indicate Olga's dominant trait: a tendency toward reflection. Her eyebrows were two "brown, fluffy, almost straight streaks that were seldom symmetrical: one was slightly higher than the other, causing a tiny wrinkle above it which seemed to say something, as if some thought rested there" (IV, 198–99); the wrinkle is also associated with tenacity (275).[5] Henceforth a simple reference to this facial detail suffices to evoke the essence of her character. Yet, the repeated motif does not limit her; on the contrary, Olga is a developing character, and she moves precisely in the direction of a more intense consciousness and a stronger will. Thus, the leading motifs suggest potentiality as much as identity. They also facilitate illuminating character comparisons and contrasts.

The most perfect integration of part and whole, physical detail and psychology, even fate, is seen in the portrayal of Oblomov. Goncharov's general description seems almost studiedly vague, stressing Oblomov's softness and the "absence of any definite idea, any concentration, in the features of his face" (IV, 7). Apart from the contrast with Olga, who has a concentrated look, the description indicates the unformed nature of Oblomov, as well as his lack of purpose. However, it is the sharply observed detail through which Oblomov becomes real. For example, his slippers were "long, soft and wide; when he put his feet out of bed onto the floor he invariably stepped straight into them without looking" (8). These details tell us a great deal about Oblomov's way of life, of habits engrained by years of lying around. A variation of this motif accompanying his decision "Now or never!" not only conveys his inner disturbance, but the insight it offers helps us to forecast his fate: "Oblomov raised himself a little from the chair, but when his feet did not find his slippers at once he sat down again" (193). It is by the repeated use of such trifles that Goncharov's best effects in character portrayal are attained and the inner structure of his work is projected.

The structural effect is one of symbolic foreshadowing, a device that occurs frequently in *Oblomov*. It is best exemplified

by the way Goncharov handles the motif of the *khalat*, the
robe. During his romance Oblomov throws off his robe, but
there are several mentions of it. Each reference awakens all
the associations of the symbolic garment; the robe, as it were,
falls like a shadow upon the future and spells doom for his
love. V. G. Korolenko pointed out an extremely subtle detail
of this sort, namely, some flies drowning in a jug of kvass in
"Oblomov's Dream." An awakened sleeper seizes the jug and
blows on the flies in preparation for drinking, "at which the
flies, hitherto motionless, began to stir intensely in the hope
of improving their situation" (IV, 116). The critic comments:

There emerges the notion of something that is still alive, capable of flying,
but already dying in an atmosphere of motionless stagnation and nightmare
sleep. . . . And you feel that the child's soul is also helplessly struggling,
trying to take wing above this realm of sleep; but already fine threads
are entangling the childish spirit in a sticky net.

One recalls how Stolz tells Oblomov he has shed his wings.
This instance of unconscious symbolism, Korolenko suggests,
not only expresses the history of Oblomov, but presents an
image of prereform Russia in general.[6]

Goncharov's art at its best makes the physical transparent,
imbuing it with psychological value or symbolic meaning. We
read the curve of Agafya's feelings for Oblomov—and in particular his response to them—in her changing waistline, and her
shrinking physique under the impact of Oblomov's death is elo-
quent of her profound grief. Oblomov's own sorrow at the loss of
Olga comes to us by way of a bleak winter landscape to which
he reacts. Generally, his inner world is revealed through everything that surrounds him, his clothing, his furniture, all the
little items that make up his daily life. This indirect psychological analysis, performed in terms of objective correlatives—objects
which acquire symbolic value—is the only one at which Goncharov excels; for he is mediocre at presenting states of mind
and internal change directly. Hence the importance of symbolic
action, the only adequate term for Oblomov's behavior in regard
to his slippers, his sofa and his robe, as well as for the elaborate
development of the lilac motif. However, the perfect mastery

of this technique does not extend beyond *Oblomov*. When used in connection with the central symbol in *The Precipice*, for example, it becomes melodramatic and approaches allegory.

Goncharov's broad use of imagery is an extension of this method, reflecting a need to give sensory form to an idea, a feeling or a mood. At times his figurative language is truly inspired, such as the bird image that evokes the whimsical quality of Oblomov's mind: "Thoughts strayed all over his face like birds, fluttered in his eyes, perched on his half-parted lips, hid in the furrows of his brow, and then vanished . . ." (IV, 7). The poetic suggestiveness of Goncharov's art is startlingly manifest in one variation of this image: "How terrible he felt . . . when, one after another, various vital questions wakened in his mind, whirling about confusedly like frightened birds roused suddenly by a ray of sunlight in a slumbering ruin" (100). The delicate vignette sketched in this extended simile has a clear meaning—the anguish of spiritual decay—but, beyond this, its inner landscape is fraught with a wide range of connotations, esthetic as well as psychological.

Goncharov knew, however, that the ever-present tension between concept and percept, idea and image, was not always so happily resolved. Occasionally he manipulated his motifs in the interest of a tendency or a program. He felt himself that even in *Oblomov* he had been overexplicit in a couple of instances, namely, in his handling of the motifs of Oblomovka and Oblomovism. At the moment of leaving the Vyborg district on his last visit, Stolz, "with a last look at the windows of the little house," says: "Goodbye, old Oblomovka! . . . Your day is over." And when Olga asks him "what is going on there," he answers, "Oblomovism" (IV, 498). Goncharov says that Stolz's parting words were unnecessary: "Oblomov explains himself sufficiently by himself, asking Stolz to *go, not to touch him,* saying that *he had grown bodily onto the old; if you tear me away I shall die!*" (VIII, 79). Furthermore, he notes that if he had seen in the image of Oblomov what "Dobrolyubov and others, and finally I myself, later found in him, I . . . would deliberately have strengthened this or that trait and, of course, would have spoiled it" (71).

The element of didacticism, of revealing too explicitly the

drift of his theme, appears mainly in dialogue and descriptions, important components of the Goncharov novel. The dialogue of educated people suffers most in this respect. The conversations of the Aduevs as well as those of Oblomov with Stolz are frankly thematic, as are too many of the exchanges in *The Precipice*. But where he has no special axe to grind and yields to the subsurface of human relationships, Goncharov shows remarkable psychological insight and the ability to give it vivid form. Thus, the bizarre tug of war between Oblomov, on the one hand, and Zakhar and Tarantiev on the other, charged with the explosive connotations of words like "venomous," "other people" and "Germans," is a wonderful shadow fencing in which the real content of these ambivalent relationships comes through in all sorts of humorous ways. The element of suggestion is strongest where an attendant action, or a gesture, undercuts the verbal exchange or the inner speech. For example, at the moment of announcing his decision not to take the new apartment, Oblomov has his eyes glued to the landlady's bosom (IV, 310). Olga's reaction to Oblomov's attempt to withdraw his involuntary love declaration illustrates the same basic pattern. While her thoughts go, "It's just as well . . . nothing to worry about now. We can talk and joke as before," her feelings run contrary: "She violently tore a twig from a tree as she walked, bit off a leaf and immediately threw both the twig and the leaf onto the path" (216–17). Indicating a sensitive awareness of the disparate strata of the psyche, these examples demonstrate an ability to present the human image in all its ambiguous complexity, unhampered by any preconceptions.

The general tension between reality and the idea affects also the larger aspects of Goncharov's fiction. An admirer of Pushkin's classical art, he consciously pursued formal harmony and shaped his novels in terms of symmetrical balance; his favorite arrangement is variations on a theme. But within this general pattern there is a great difference between *A Common Story*, with its linear structure, strict composition and rather skimpy substance, and the almost excessive plenitude of *Oblomov*, where his talent and his thought approach a state of harmony. In *The Precipice* the formal scheme is wider and the many parallel actions make it abundant with vivid life; however, as we have shown, ideas of a nonesthetic kind inflict damaging flaws upon the novel. The precarious balance has collapsed.

II   *The Source and Nature of Goncharov's Inspiration*

In commenting on his own work Goncharov stressed its objective aspects, claiming that he had written a trilogy describing three periods of Russian life, "the old life, *sleep*, and *awakening*" (VIII, 162). On the other hand he says he wrote only about his own life and about "*what had grown onto it*" (113). The truth is that his work oscillates between many extremes, self and society, subjectivity and objectivity, contemporary history and the eternal problems of man.

Goncharov's concept of the novel was very broad. Raysky, comparing it to the ocean, says "all of life can be put into the novel, both as a whole and in its parts" (V, 41–42). Goncharov's creative experience fully agrees with this concept. He says that he never envisaged one action; instead, "all at once there opened before my eyes, as from a mountain, an entire region with towns, villages, forests, and with a crowd of people—in short, a large sphere of a full, integral life."[7] But while he formulates a panoramic concept of the novel, he does not see the author as a mere recorder of phenomena. As against the cold observation that he found in the products of the "new Realist school," he champions the rights of the imagination and the heart in literature. Nature, he says, cannot be represented directly: "From a direct snapshot of it one gets only a pitiful, feeble copy. It allows itself to be approached only by way of the creative imagination." As other "powerful instruments of art" he mentions humor and typicality, "in short, poetry" (VIII, 108), in another context also "feeling" (211). A mouthpiece for the author in "A Literary Evening" says that "the living connection between the artist and his work should be felt by the spectator or the reader; they, so to speak, enjoy the picture with the help of the author's feelings . . ." (VII, 157). Despite his dispassionate narrative manner, Goncharov did not seek to express the nature of reality apart from his own attitudes. Without being an impressionist, he assumes that in art reality is refracted through a temperament.

While "memory" cannot form part of a literary work in the same way as "feeling" or "humor," it can certainly color it, whether with retrospective pleasure or pain, nostalgia or disenchantment. Though Goncharov never directly mentions the role of memory in his writing, its importance is quite clear from scattered comments in his letters and essays as well as from the novels themselves. Leon Stilman in particular stresses the retrospective quality of his fiction, ascribing to it a "chronology of memory."[8] Just as his heroes experience the healing or consoling effects of spontaneous memory—whether Alexander Aduev during his stay at Grachi, Oblomov in his recapture of his childhood, or Raysky on his visit to Malinovka—so Goncharov as a writer seems to have drawn largely upon his own store of personal memories, sealed within the chambers of his mind. His account of the inception of *The Precipice* suggests that the spark of creation came from a collision between his old memories of his birthplace and the new impressions received on his visit home in 1849. He writes: "Here old, familiar faces gushed up in a crowd. . . . The gardens, the Volga, the steeps on its banks, the native air, childhood recollections—all this was deposited in my head and nearly prevented me from completing *Oblomov* . . ." (VIII, 71-72). For the task of artistically shaping this vision, retained over the years, absolute quiet was an "indispensable" condition (358). Goncharov's inspiration, seemingly rooted in a profound nostalgia for the vanishing old life, was as intimate as that of Proust in his cork-lined room.

This is also evident from the reflection of the author's deepest preoccupations in his heroes, formed around the contrast between youth and maturity, romanticism and sober adjustment. Interestingly, he says at one time that they are all "one person being successively reborn" (VIII, 162). The "evil sickness" of romanticism associated with his youth never ceased to interest him, and romantics of one kind or another were always at the center of his novels; Raysky is especially close to his creator and fails as a character largely because of lack of esthetic distance. But while Goncharov is unreasonably attached to the failures he shows up, probably because the old order of life to which they belong is seen in a golden haze of reminiscence, the mature, pragmatic representatives of an emerging capitalistic civilization who have his intellectual assent are subtly discredited, in particular through their shortcomings as husbands or lovers. These ambivalences manifest Goncharov's deep involvement in his work. Wholly contented with neither world, in the words of one critic his response to life was tinged with the "unsatisfied yearning of the chosen."[9]

To Goncharov writing was an act of self-knowledge, as it is to Raysky (VI, 206). Seemingly indifferent after a certain age to acquire new experience, he expressed in his novels—all incidentally dating back to the 1840's—a personal vision of life. But this does not mean that his fiction "reflected little but the various aspects of his own personality."[10] Goncharov often refers to the transforming power of the imagination, whereby what is personal by derivation acquires a broader significance. It has been suggested that his greatest claim to immortality is precisely his ability to generalize the results of self-observation and thus give a "truly objective picture of his society."[11] Through his gift of artistic generalization, Goncharov expanded his narrow world of "observations, impressions and memories" (VIII, 113) to embrace typical phenomena not only of his own age, but of human life at all times.

III *The Fictional World of Goncharov*

From his early years Goncharov was familiar mostly with the life of the middle landed gentry and the patriarchal merchants (*kuptsy*), and it is the calm rhythms of the life of these social groups, in its phases of evolution and decline, that lie at the basis of his work. Though St. Petersburg is important as a setting, it does not affect the style and form of his fiction, as it did in the case of Gogol and Dostoevsky.

The rhythm of Goncharov's novels is attuned to the slow tides of organic change, within a recurring cycle of life. Oblomov's existence at Vyborg, we recall, is paced by geological time, which works with imperceptible slowness: only the *effects* of change are noted. This is also Goncharov's procedure when he shows human life and experience against the background of the seasons; he presents a series of significant moments, making change perceptible through the differences between succes-

sive stages. This procedure is explained by his talent, which is
best at rendering a settled order of things, stasis; one critic
correctly points out his delight in still life.[12]

Violent change, with which society was rife in the 1860's
when he was writing *The Precipice*, he simply considered unfit
for literary treatment in the novel form. The "new life," being
caught in a "process of ferment," could only be reflected in the
"mirror of satire, the light sketch, and not in large epic works"
(VIII, 80); its heroes, living only "in theory" (161), had not
crystalized a recognizable way of life. Actually, he saw such
attempts at breaking with the past merely as eddies in the
stream of life that soon merge back into the main current.
His thinking on this score is typified by the opening sentences
of a chapter subsequent to Vera's fall: "The days passed by
and once more brought stillness to hover above Malinovka.
Once again life, held back by catastrophe like a river by rapids,
broke through the barrier and flowed on, more calmly" (VI,
347). Passion, as well as social rebellion, is an aberration within
such a context, where every transition is gradual. At the end of
The Precipice life is renewed from the best of the old—so, at
least, is the intent.

Goncharov's dislike of violent change is related to his artistic
aim, namely, to "illuminate all the depths of life, lay bare its
hidden bases and whole mechanism" (VIII, 212), a task that
can be realized only when life is fairly stable. Within this
ambitious project the focal point is man as embedded in an
order proceeding from several generations, even centuries; nature
is important chiefly as it conforms to, or reflects, this life. One
reason why Goncharov admired the playwright Ostrovsky was
the broad temporal reach of his work, which he called a
"millennial monument to Russia" (VIII, 179). His own span
was narrow by comparison, but the life he describes best is
always that which has endured for a long time and therefore
has assumed a finished form—the life of Oblomovka and Malinovka. Merezhkovsky speaks of a "poetry of the past,"[13] stressing
Goncharov's ability to draw the completed forms of reality.
Appropriately enough, Goncharov defined a literary type in
terms of recurrence: "a type is made up of many and long
repetitions or accumulations of phenomena and persons, where

the similarities of both become more frequent in the course of time and finally become established . . ." (457). Thus he presents entire eras and orders of life rather than the changing profiles of successive decades as implied in his notion of having produced a trilogy.

Within any order of life, in Goncharov's organic view, the old and the new meet. In terms of his own world, the impact of European civilization had introduced a seed of change into the patriarchal order of Russian life. A moderate Westernist deeply attached to the old Russian ways, he attempts to reconcile the conflicting forces. However, these forces are unequally portrayed. While the representatives of the old order, especially Oblomov, are shown in the round, the antagonists are pale ideal figures without depth. Significantly, his attempts to catch or stem the drift of the future in such characters as Stolz, Tushin, and Volokhov are contrary to his literary theory, which required esthetic distance and assumed the impossibility of describing the "process of [contemporary] ferment." Tushin and Stolz are ideal solutions to the problem of change rather than living embodiments of new social forces.

The resulting polarity is related to a permanent bifurcation in Goncharov's esthetic thrust, divided between his eye upon the object and his own inner needs. As a keen observer he is—in Schillerian language—a "naïve" writer who finds reality to be an adequate object of representation; but as a thinker, intent upon what ought to be, he is a "sentimental" writer and tries to improve upon reality by creating esthetic embodiments of ideas and ideals.[14] With a self-confessed longing for a "beautiful image of man" (VIII, 258),[15] he was unable to embody it without violating his most fundamental tenet, expressed in Belinsky's formula "thinking in images." In his endeavor to create works of art that would help to "crown education and perfect man" (VIII, 211)—an aim that, according to Raysky, is the sine qua non of progress (VI, 8)—he was no more successful than others before him. Quite understandably; for how could "humor" and "poetry" be made to serve the moral perfection of man? Though he wished to offer a positive hero, he was incapable of showing him from within or of giving him his affection. With all "feeling" and "poetry," along with most of

the "imagination," expended upon the nonhero, Oblomov, how
can Stolz, however valiant, compete? And how can Tushin, the
lumber king, be a match for Volokhov, who, however maligned,
has the advantage of being loved by the beautiful heroine?

Only in portraying the life he knew and loved best was
Goncharov able to follow his deepest artistic insights. Here, in
the words of Dobrolyubov, he is able to "grasp the complete
image of an object . . . [,] to halt the fleeting phenomenon of
life in all its fullness and freshness." Dobrolyubov's characterization of Goncharov's distinguishing trait as a novelist has been
unjustly neglected in favor of his thesis of the "superfluous man";
it still provides the best description of his artistic profile. Stressing the "calm and completeness" of his poetic perception, the
critic notes that Goncharov "is not struck by one aspect of an
object, one moment of an event; he turns the object around
full circle and waits until all the moments of a phenomenon
have occurred. . . ." He does not let go of an object until he
has "discovered its causes and understood its connections with
all the phenomena surrounding it."[16] Interestingly, Dobrolyubov
echoes a thought that Goncharov expressed in a letter of 1857
while he was working on *Oblomov*. He says that with him the
main thing is not the style, but "the completeness and finish of
the whole structure." He fears that Oblomov may be an "incom-
plete" character, that some aspect or other may be missing or
not related; but he hopes the reader will supply the missing
items from his own imagination. Only Cervantes said all, he
adds, and not without some boredom (VIII, 291).

Also, Goncharov and Dobrolyubov both refer to the psychological aspect of the picture of life. The critic writes that "the
very inwardness, the soul, of every person and of every object"
is revealed.[17] Speaking of *The Precipice*, Goncharov notes that
descriptions of manners and morals "never make a profound
impression unless at the same time they touch man himself,
his psychological aspect" (VIII, 159). Though he is very modest
about his own accomplishment in this regard, he makes it clear
that it was part of his task. The important words here are "man
himself," as against the collective image of life which Goncharov
evokes with such apparent ease.

In his endeavor to combine the broad picture of life with

psychological depth, Goncharov followed the example of some of the greatest writers of the past. We know that, apart from Pushkin and Gogol, his masters were Shakespeare, Cervantes and Molière (VIII, 108); these were his models of realism. Cervantes was more to him than a paragon of esthetic completeness. Don Quixote and Hamlet, in his view, embodied "almost everything that is comic and tragic in human nature" (366). One notes the similarities between Goncharov's structural principles and the clashing perspectives, of faith and scepticism, action and contemplation, self and society, which lie at the basis of *Don Quixote* and of *Hamlet*. The crucial importance of these works to Goncharov may be due to historical coincidence: both Shakespeare and Cervantes reflect a culture in transition from feudalism to the modern age, and two hundred and fifty years later Goncharov found himself in a country undergoing a comparable change. This makes his fiction contemporary in a new, broader sense, and retrospectively historical, just as *Don Quixote* and *Hamlet* can be said to be historical. Lyatsky may have had something like this in mind when he called his work a "living reflection of the historical moment."[18] At the same time, his practice of juxtaposing his own characters with heroic figures like those just mentioned, or with Don Juan and Faust, gives them a wider amplitude. For whether it dwarfs or dignifies, this device places his characters, especially Oblomov, on a line with some of the supreme literary archetypes of all time, and the juxtaposition suggests that, however different, they struggle with the same eternal questions faced by their illustrious counterparts. Similar in effect to the mythic method, this technique is less rigorous, working through an allusive style which sets up a series of mock-mirrors or virtual parallels.

IV *Goncharov's Position as a Novelist*

The significance of Goncharov in the Russian and European novel is very great. For in the course of chronicling the old life he created a fictional form of striking originality. Starting out by parodying the fashionable stories in vogue in the 1830's and going on to the physiological sketch, he produced in *Oblomov* a work which set a landmark in the Russian novel. He

was the first Russian to develop the novel to a point at which
it became comparable in esthetic stature to the ancient epic,
by its magnitude, complexity, national relevance, and poetic
quality. Compared to Goncharov, Turgenev becomes a writer
of novelettes. And though Tolstoy worked on a much broader
scale, his novels are less poetic.

We have used the word "poetic" before in discussing *Oblomov*
and *The Precipice*. In *The Modern Psychological Novel* Leon
Edel devotes a chapter to "The Novel as Poem," showing that
"the stream of consciousness novel approaches the condition
of poetry."[19] In a different form this quality was anticipated by
certain nineteenth-century writers, of whom Goncharov is one
of the most important. *Oblomov*, to choose his best work, is
marked by a far more intimate interweaving of parts and of
the compositional elements than we find in most contemporary
novels; Dostoevsky's best work has this quality, as does Chekhov's. "Poetic" is here used in the sense of organic structure,
in which every part is interrelated with every other, bringing
the texture of language to a level of complexity and richness
which is characteristic of good verse.

To illustrate, setting in Goncharov's work, whether landscapes
or interiors, becomes interlaced with man and turns into a
source of changing symbols of human experience. Moreover,
through the use of motifs, plot is supplemented by another,
nonlinear, principle of structure, which sets up rhythms and
counterrhythms in time. The use of motifs also means that the
story is partly conveyed by suggestion, another method associated more with poetry than with prose. Finally, Goncharov's
language displays image clusters of considerable consistency,
sometimes with archetypal connotations. That he was unable
to repeat the triumph of *Oblomov* is deplorable; but in any
case, like so many great novels of our own time *The Precipice*
was intended as a symbolic embodiment of the author's own
experience, possibly the reason why Goncharov had a special
affection for it.

The techniques and qualities just mentioned are all such as
came to the forefront only after the turn of the century, when
Thomas Mann, James Joyce, and Marcel Proust entered upon
the literary scene. Yet, Goncharov's work also fits into the con-

text of European literature of his day. Indeed, it acquires its full meaning only when seen in this context.

The novel of disillusionment which Goncharov cultivated flourished in France for several decades after the Restoration. Among famous works, aside from Balzac's *Lost Illusions* discussed in connection with *A Common Story*, Flaubert's *Madame Bovary* (1857), published two years before *Oblomov*, belongs to this category. Goncharov's affinity with Flaubert has frequently been noted. Strange as it may sound, *Madame Bovary* and *Oblomov* have quite a few things in common.

Both are stories of disillusionment and of the total destruction of personality, though in different modes. Emma, like Oblomov, is tainted by romanticism—pseudo-romanticism in her case, decadent romanticism in his. An almost total alienation occurs between their private worlds and the society around them. As in the case of Oblomov, despite her many failings we feel attracted to Emma, who, if we disregard Charles's rather bovine integrity, is the only character in the book with a modicum of aspiration. And, without sounding too false a note, Goncharov could probably have said, *"Oblomov—c'est moi!"* Moreover, both writers were equally concerned with the niceties of style. Goncharov's style combines the spontaneity of an improvisation with meticulous workmanship. To illustrate the latter, in his letter to Olga, Oblomov uses the phrase "fragrant memory" (IV, 260), an adjective which seems deliberately chosen by the author to echo the flower symbolism of the "poem of love."

At the same time there are obvious differences between the two novels: the treatment of Oblomov is less objective and ironic, alternating between humor and lyricism and avoiding the more sordid naturalistic details. Too, the antagonists differ greatly. Homais, the pharmacist who receives the medal of the Legion of Honor at the end of *Madame Bovary*, is an ironically treated Philistine, and one wonders whether Goncharov's book would not have profited by meting out a similar treatment to Stolz. By compensation, *Oblomov* is superior in poetic value.

While Flaubert and *Madame Bovary* have influenced the modern novel much more.[20] *Oblomov* stands just as close to the structural principles and esthetic qualities of the great

works of fiction of our century. Its literary value to us is twofold:
formally, it combines a structure of monumental simplicity with
an intricate imagistic texture; in terms of substance it presents
a hero who unites idiosyncratic traits with class, national and
universal characteristics in tragicomic synthesis. The depth and
charm of this figure is amply proven by the fact that, in 1963
and 1964, two different plays based on *Oblomov* were running
on Paris and London stages respectively. As long as literary
art will be valued for its intrinsic merit, Oblomov will continue
to enact his slow rise and fall before our eyes, evoking our
bemused wonder, pity, and laughter at the vagaries of the
human heart.

Notes and References

Preface
1. See "O prichinakh upadka i o novykh techeniiakh sovremennoi russkoi literatury," in *Polnoe sobranie sochinenii,* XV (St. Petersburg-Moscow, 1912), 252–54.

Chapter One
1. I. A. Goncharov, *Sobranie sochinenii* (Collected Works), with an Introd. by S. M. Petrov, 8 vols. (Moscow, 1952–55), IV, 503. Subsequent references to this publication will be included in the text, with indication of volume number and page unless the former is evident from the context.
2. Letter of July 15, 1865 as quoted by A. P. Rybasov, *I. A. Goncharov* (Moscow, 1962), p. 29.
3. *Ibid.,* p. 30.
4. From Druzhinin's unpublished diary as quoted by A. G. Tseitlin, *I. A. Goncharov* (Moscow, 1950), p. 219. (Unspaced periods are part of the quoted text, spaced periods indicate omission.)
5. As quoted by Tseitlin, *ibid.,* p. 20.
6. Rybasov, *op. cit.,* p. 12.
7. It is Raysky in *The Precipice,* however, who most fully reflects Goncharov's negative reaction to the world in which he grew up, as well as the compensations offered by the vicarious experiences of reading.
8. Rybasov, *loc. cit.*
9. "Oblomovka Revisited," *American Slavic and East European Review,* VI (1948), 69.
10. *Neobyknovennaia istoriia,* in *Sbornik Rossiiskoi Publichnoi biblioteki,* II, No. 1 (Petrograd, 1924), pp. 7–189.
11. There is evidence of extensive psychopathology in Goncharov's family, affecting his father, his brother, and one of his sisters. (See André Mazon, *Un maître du roman russe: Ivan Gontcharov* [Paris, 1914], pp. 6, 240.) Goncharov himself speaks of his suspiciousness as an "inborn and hereditary malady" transmitted from his mother (VIII, 409).
12. The view of V. F. Pereverzev, argued on the premises of Marxist

168   IVAN GONCHAROV

sociologism, that Goncharov's gentlemen of the gentry are masks for bourgeois types representing different stages of development of the Russian bourgeoisie, has not been widely accepted. For Pereverzev's view, see in particular "Sotsial'nyi genezis oblomovshchiny," *Pechat' i revoliutsiia*, 1925, No. 2, pp. 61–78, and "K voprosu o monisticheskom ponimanii tvorchestva Goncharova," in *Literaturovedenie: Sbornik statei,* ed. V. F. Pereverzev (Moscow, 1928), pp. 201–29; for criticism and rebuttal, see B. Neumann, "Die Gontscharow-Forschung von 1918–1928," *Zeitschrift für slavische Philologie,* VII (1930), 170–72, and V. Desnitskii, "Trilogiia Goncharova," in *Izbrannye stat'i po russkoi literature 18–19 vekov* (M.–L., 1958), pp. 291–332.

Chapter Two

1. *Goncharov: Zhizn', lichnost', tvorchestvo,* 3. ed., pp. 323–55.

2. In the series *Nedra,* X (Moscow, 1927), 243–82.

3. I. A. Goncharov, *Literaturno-kriticheskie stat'i i pis'ma,* ed. A. P. Rybasov (Leningrad, 1938), p. 337.

4. As late as 1874, in his "Notes on the Personality of Belinsky," Goncharov stands up for his late friend Benediktov (d. 1873), about whose talent he used to disagree with Belinsky (VIII, 55). For all that, A. Rybasov surmises (*op. cit.,* p. 35) that the "crushing blow" which Belinsky dealt the poetry of Benediktov in an article of 1835 may have opened Goncharov's eyes to the worthlessness of his own verse.

5. The poems were published in 1938 (*Zvezda,* no. 5, pp. 243–46), with a brief commentary by A. Rybasov.

6. In an article in *Russkaia literatura* for 1960 (No. 1, pp. 39–44) the Soviet critic O. Demikhovskaia argues, mainly on stylistic grounds, that Goncharov wrote an earlier story, "Nimfodora Ivanovna," which appeared, without signature or initials, in supplements to two successive issues of *Podsnezhnik* ("The Snowdrop") for 1836. This attribution is apparently accepted by A. D. Alekseev, who lists the item both in his chronicle and his bibliography of Goncharov. However, we have been informed by the Institute of Russian Literature in Leningrad (IRLI), where the manuscript (f. 168, No. 16494. CU. b. 1. 1. 126–75) is kept, that many Goncharov specialists consider his authorship "extremely doubtful." After reading the story, graciously made available to us in microfilm by Dr. N. V. Izmaylov, we cannot help agreeing with this judgment. However, the story has already been published as Goncharov's by Demikhovskaia, who in 1968 had it printed in the weekly supplement to *Izvestiia* (Nos. 1-3).

7. In his autobiographical sketch of 1858 Goncharov alludes rather condescendingly to certain stories of "domestic content, that is, such as related to private affairs and people, on the humorous side and in no way remarkable" (VIII, 223).

8. I. A. Goncharov, *Povesti i ocherki*, ed. B. M. Engel'gardt (Leningrad, 1937), p. 20. Subsequent references will appear in the text.

9. Goncharov was quite candid about his own, and others', indebtedness to Pushkin and Gogol. In *Better Late Than Never* (written in the 1870's) he alleges that all subsequent writers of fiction have only further developed "the material bequeathed by them" (VIII, 76). "Pushkin, I say, was our teacher—and I was brought up, so to speak, on his poetry. Gogol influenced me much later and less; I had begun writing myself before Gogol's career came to an end" (77). Goncharov's early acquaintance with Sterne is indicated in his third autobiographical sketch (228).

10. Rybasov, *op. cit.*, pp. 41–42.

11. For an interesting discussion of the physiological sketch, see A. G. Tseitlin's posthumously published work *Stanovlenie realizma v russkoi literature* (Moscow, 1965).

12. See *The Inspector General*, Act III, Scene vi.—Podzhabrin's opening formula runs, with minor variations: "At last I am with you! Can it really be true? Or am I dreaming?" (VII, 26).

13. Cf. Northrop Frye's statement to the effect that "the more ironic the comedy, the more absurd the society." (*Anatomy of Criticism* [Princeton, 1957], p. 176.)

14. *Ibid.*

15. Introduction to I. A. Goncharov, *Povesti i ocherki*, p. 7.

Chapter Three

1. *Polnoe sobranie sochinenii*, XII (Moscow, 1956), 352.

2. V. Burenin, "Romanist prezhnego vremeni," in *Kriticheskie etiudy* (St. Petersburg, 1888), p. 76.

3. Belinsky called this ending "unnatural and false." The critic sensed the profound temperamental differences between uncle and nephew, and believed the latter should have been left in the "rustic wilderness" to perish in "apathy and idleness," or even better, he might be made into that "quite modern romantic," a Slavophile. (*I. A. Goncharov v russkoi kritike* [Moscow, 1951], pp. 50–51.) By contrast, Dostoevsky in *The Underground Man* conceives of the Russian romantic as a breed capable of the most base materialism (Pt. IX, ch. 1).

4. A. I. Herzen, *Sobranie sochinenii*, III (Moscow, 1954), 24–42.

5. *Poln. sobr. soch.*, VI (1955), 524. Tseitlin (*I. A. Goncharov*, p. 62) sees a literal echo of this idea of two extremes in the author's comment that Lizaveta "was the witness of two terrible extremes in her nephew and uncle. One was rhapsodic to the point of madness, the other cold to the point of hardness" (I, 151).

6. *Poln. sobr. soch.*, VIII (1955), 396.

7. *Ibid.*, VI, 672.

8. Young Aduev refers to his having translated Schiller (I, 58); Goncharov did the same in his early youth (see his *Literaturno-kriticheskie stat'i i pis'ma*, p. 337).

9. A study by Clarence A. Manning is relevant in this connection. By relating the chronology of *A Common Story* to Russian history, Manning shows the lack of historical perspective in the novel. He claims that Goncharov was "singularly untouched by the agitation and the developments of his day." "The Neglect of Time in the Russian Novel," *Slavic Studies*, ed. Alexander Kaun & Ernest J. Simmons (Ithaca, 1943), pp. 109–10.

10. "Goncharov," *op. cit.*, XIII: *Vechnye sputniki* (St. Petersburg-Moscow, 1911), p. 241.

11. In making translations of phrases for illustration, we have not necessarily chosen the best form of expression all around, but the one which best brings out the point under discussion.

12. In creating Peter, the author may have drawn upon the world of bureaucrats in which he moved. The theme of "active work" of which the uncle is the representative was, he says, "reflected by my little mirror in the intermediate ranks of the bureaucracy" (VIII, 73). For a discussion of possible models both for Peter and for other figures in *A Common Story*, see Tseitlin, *I. A. Goncharov*, p. 57.

13. James M. Edie et al., eds. *Russian Philosophy* (Chicago, 1965), I, 276.

14. André Mazon (*op. cit.*, pp. 70, 318, 325) has pointed out a possible indebtedness to Balzac's *The Physiology of Marriage* (1829) in this connection.

15. *Hard Times*, Norton Critical Edition (New York, 1966), p. 167.

16. Mazon, *op. cit.*, p. 50.

17. See the reminiscence of G. N. Potanin in *I. A. Goncharov v vospominaniiakh sovremennikov* (Leningrad, 1969), p. 24.

18. A. S. Pushkin, *Stikhotvoreniia*, ed. B. Meilakh, 3rd ed., Biblioteka poeta, Malaia seriia (Leningrad, 1954), I, 387.

19. *Ibid.*, p. 389.

20. *Ibid.*, p. 388.

21. *Ibid.*, p. 233.

22. See *Collected Works*, I, pp. 45, 101, 152, 247.

23. It is worth noting that Belinsky thought the alternate fate, that of a Philistine, the only possible one for Lensky. This view was expressed in Part VIII of his Pushkin critique; it was printed in *Notes of the Fatherland* for December, 1844, in the same year that Goncharov worked out the plan for his novel. See *Poln. sobr. soch.*, VII (1955), 472.

24. Pushkin, *op. cit.*, III, 224.

25. For comments on these possibilities as well as parallels with other French novels, see Mazon, *op. cit.,* pp. 73–75, 312–14, 317–18.

26. René Marchand, *Parallèles littéraires franco-russes* (Mexico, Escuela normal superior, 1949), p. 136.

27. For an interesting interpretation of this novel, see Georg Lukács, *Studies in European Realism* (New York, 1964), pp. 47–64.

Chapter Four

1. Piotr A. Kropotkin, *Ideals and Realities in Russian Literature* (New York, 1915), p. 159.

2. *Neobyknovennaia istoriia,* in *op. cit.,* p. 129.

3. V. S. Pritchett, "The Great Absentee," in *The Living Novel* (London, 1946), p. 235.

4. Tarantiev's name, derived from *tarantit'* or *taranta,* both with the root meaning of glib, empty talk, suggests a "windbag."

5. Georg Lukács, *Die Theorie des Romans,* 2nd ed. (Berlin, 1963), p. 123.

6. A. V. Druzhinin, in *I. A. Goncharov v russkoi kritike,* p. 166.

7. This distinction is very close to one made in the brief sketch "Khorosho ili durno zhit' na svete," written by Goncharov in the early 1840's after several visits to the Catherine Institute, a boarding school for girls. See Tseitlin, *I. A. Goncharov,* pp. 445–49.

8. Cf. Goncharov's laconic reaction to a storm at sea: "Hideousness, disorder!" (II, 255). He says he could never understand "the poetry of the sea" (II, 40).

9. "Apology," in *The Dialogues of Plato,* tr. B. Jowett, with an Introduction by R. Demos (New York, 1937), I, 420.

10. *Cosmos and History: The Myth of the Eternal Return,* tr. Willard R. Trask (New York, 1959), p. 35.

11. *Ibid.,* p. 36.

12. N. I. Prutskov, *Masterstvo Goncharova-romanista* (M.-L., 1962), p. 110.

13. There is a striking similarity between Agafya Matveyevna's name and patronymic, and those of Goncharov's own mother, Avdotya Matveyevna. Whatever inferences one wishes to draw from this, it may be noted that, externally, Oblomov's relationship with Agafya reflects the connection between the gentleman N. N. Tregubov and Mrs. Goncharov. As already indicated, Tregubov for many years had a common household with Goncharov's mother.

14. *Polnoe sobranie sochinenii i pisem,* XIV (Moscow, 1949), 354.

15. Kropotkin, *op. cit.,* p. 155.

16. *I. A. Goncharov v russkoi kritike,* p. 38.

17. This no doubt reflects Goncharov's own feeling for Elizabeth Tolstoy, whom he courted assiduously for a brief period in 1855. The many coincidences between Oblomov's language and the images, thoughts, and feelings occurring in Goncharov's correspondence with Elizabeth Tolstoy (*Golos minuvshego*, 1913, No. 11, pp. 215–35, & No. 12, pp. 222–52) conclusively show that Goncharov's personal torment found sublimated expression in *Oblomov*. (See P. Sakulin, "Novaia glava iz biografii I. A. Goncharova v neizdannykh pis'makh," *Golos minuvshego*, 1913, No. 11, pp. 45–65.) However, O. Chemena denies that Elizabeth Tolstoy was the prototype for Olga, claiming this distinction for Catherine P. Maykov, to whom Goncharov was deeply devoted. (*"Oblomov* I. A. Goncharova i Ekaterina Maikova," *Russkaia literatura*, 1959, No. 3, pp. 159–68.)

18. *I. A. Goncharov v russkoi kritike*, p. 102.

19. *Ibid.*, p. 66.

20. *Istoriia russkoi intelligentsii*, Pt. I, 6th ed., in *Sobranie sochinenii* (Moscow, 1923–24), VII, 210–11.

21. "I. A. Goncharov," *Vestnik Evropy*, 1912, No. 6, pp. 209–10.

22. *Istoriia russkoi intelligentsii*, p. 217. This trait is interesting in view of current American usage in regard to the term "Oblomovism." A review of a book about Senator Eugene McCarthy in *Time* (March 2, 1970, p. 78) headed "Oblomov for President" speaks of the Senator's "acedia, his spiritual Oblomovism." "He [McCarthy] emerges from these pages as an almost hermetically private man."

23. *Ibid.*, p. 220. In varying formulations, this characterization of Oblomovism has a long history. Druzhinin says that Oblomovism is in the same relation to everyday life that conservatism is to politics (*I. A. Goncharov v russkoi kritike*, p. 179); Kropotkin equates Oblomov with the conservative type, "in the sense of the conservatism of well-being" (*op. cit.*, p. 160); and Renato Poggioli speaks in positive terms of Oblomov as the "personal symbol . . . of what Karamzin used to call . . . [Russia's] 'historical patience'." ("On Goncharov and His *Oblomov*," in *The Phoenix and the Spider* [Cambridge, Mass., 1957], p. 47.)

24. V. I. Lenin, *O literature i iskusstve*, 2nd ed. (Moscow, 1960), p. 479.

25. V. S. Pritchett, *op. cit.*, p. 239.

26. L. Ganchikov, "In tema di 'Oblomovismo'," *Ricerche slavistiche*, IV (1955–56), 175.

27. Stilman, *op. cit.*, p. 66.

28. A French critic, stressing Oblomov's "weaning complex," sees a "symbol of the return to prenatal life" in the way Oblomov is fed at Vyborg by a "bare arm" being thrust through the door (Pt. III, ch. 3); he also suggests that the robe is a womb symbol. François de Labriolle, "Oblomov n'est-il qu'un paresseux?," *Cahiers du monde russe et soviétique*, X (1969), No. 1, pp. 48, 50–51.

29. Stilman, *op. cit.*, p. 68.

30. *Ibid.*, p. 63.

31. "Oblomov as Anti-Faust," *Western Humanities Review*, XXI (1967), 152.

32. Review of David Magarshack's translation of *Oblomov*, in *The New Statesman and Nation*, No. 20, 1954, p. 661.

33. Dostoevsky seems to have been aware of the similarity between the two heroes and is reported to have commented upon it in conversation: "And my 'Idiot,' you know, is also an Oblomov. . . . Only, my idiot is better than Goncharov's. Goncharov's idiot is petty; there is a great deal of Philistinism in him, while my idiot is noble, elevated." M. A. Aleksandrov, "Dostoevskii v vospominaniiakh tipografskogo naborshchika v 1872–1881 godakh," *Russkaia starina*, LXXIV (1892), No. 3, p. 308.

34. N. Akhsharumov, "*Oblomov*. Roman I. Goncharova. 1859," *Russkii vestnik*, XXV (1860), No. 2, pp. 614, 625, 621.

35. Orest Miller, *Russkie pistateli posle Gogolia*, 3rd ed. (St. Petersburg, 1886), II, 18.

36. *I. A. Goncharov v russkoi kritike,* p. 91.

37. The real thrust of the action, in one critic's view, is a complete triumph of the social forces of Stolzism. It is not for nothing, he notes, that it is Stolz who pronounces Oblomov's death sentence ("Goodbye, old Oblomovka! . . .") and that Stolz takes over his bride, his estate and finally his son. V. E. Evgen'ev-Maksimov, *I. A. Goncharov* (Moscow, 1925), pp. 86–88.

38. V. S. Pritchett suggests that the "dreaded abyss" in Oblomov's love scenes with Olga is sex (*The New Statesman and Nation*, Nov. 20, 1954, p. 662); certainly, Oblomov's fear of sexual passion is evident throughout.

39. Dante Alighieri, *The Inferno,* The Temple Classics (London, 1946), p. 79.

40. For discussion of parallels and influences, see Mazon, *op. cit.*, pp. 158–63; Tseitlin, *I. A. Goncharov*, pp. 152–53; Prutskov, *op. cit.*, pp. 85–90; Desnitskii, *op. cit.*, pp. 296–303; and N. K. Piksanov, "Goncharov," in *Istoriia russkoi literatury*, VIII, Pt. 1 (M.-L., 1956), p. 450.

Chapter Five

1. O. M. Chemena, "Etapy tvorcheskoi istorii romana I. Goncharova *Obryv*," *Russkaia literatura*, 1961, No. 4, pp. 195–96.

2. *Ibid.*, p. 197.

3. See *Neobyknovennaia istoriia,* in *op. cit.*, pp. 14–15.

4. Chemena, *op. cit.*, p. 202.

5. *Ibid.*, p. 205.

6. It is hardly mere coincidence that the dénouement of *The Precipice* came to Goncharov shortly after Catherine Maykov, his intimate friend,

abandoned her husband and children to live with a Nihilist, the student Lyubimov.

7. As quoted by A. D. Alekseev in *Letopis' zhizni i tvorchestva I. A. Goncharova* (M.-L., 1960), p. 184, from manuscript materials in the Pushkin House, Leningrad.

8. *Ibid.*, p. 193.

9. See *Love in the Western World* (New York, 1957), especially the chapter entitled "The Myth is Popularized," pp. 240-44.

10. The notion of the "perversion" of passion suggests Charles Fourier's well-known concept of the "récurrences passionnelles," though the latter was more socially oriented. For comment, see N. K. Piksanov, *Roman Goncharova "Obryv" v svete sotsial'noi istorii* (Leningrad, 1968), p. 166.

11. This dedication was originally intended for *The Precipice* itself. See *M. M. Stasiulevich i ego sovremenniki v ikh perepiske* (St. Petersburg, 1912-13), IV, 10.

12. I. Turgenev, "Gamlet i Don Kikhot," in *Sobranie sochinenii*, XI (Moscow, 1956), 168-86.

13. Note Goncharov's statement in "Intentions . . ." to the effect that, "in the struggle of her character with his, she came out the victor, without giving up fundamental convictions in the matter of religion, or in her ideas of good, honesty, and honor. Morally, she stood her ground" (VIII, 218).

14. See, for example, M. E. Saltykov-Shchedrin, "Ulichnaia filosofia," in *I. A. Goncharov v russkoi kritike*, pp. 212-14.

15. Goncharov characterizes the resolution of the plot of *The Precipice* by these words in *Neobyknovennaia istoriia* (*op. cit.*, p. 143).

16. V. P. Botkin, as quoted by A. A. Fet in *Moi vospominaniia* ("My Reminiscences"), II (Moscow, 1890), 196.

17. One of the first to do so was A. V. Druzhinin in his review article on *Oblomov;* see *I. A. Goncharov v russkoi kritike*, p. 166.

18. It may be noted that as a young man Goncharov wrote a feuilleton about etiquette, with descriptions of the dandy, the man of the world, the well-bred man, and the gentleman. *Ocherki i povesti*, pp. 157-81.

19. *Studies in European Realism*, p. 171.

20. Kropotkin, *op. cit.*, p. 162.

21. Available in Tseitlin, *I. A. Goncharov*, pp. 473-76.

22. Goncharov admits, however, that he borrowed some traits both for her and other characters in the novel from people he knew on the Volga (VIII, 103). For identification of those concerned, see *I. A. Goncharov v vospominaniiakh sovremennikov*, p. 104. O. Chemena claims that the early "sterile" image of Vera received some "human" traits from Catherine Maykov ("I. A. Goncharov i semeinaia drama Maikovykh," in *Voprosy izucheniia russkoi literatury XI-XX vekov* [M.-L., 1958], p. 189). For rebuttal of

Chemena's claims, see Piksanov, *Roman Goncharova "Obryv"* . . . , pp. 190–98.

23. According to O. Chemena ("Etapy . . . ," p. 198) this part was written as early as 1856–57, that is, before the publication of *Oblomov*.

24. *Larousse Encyclopedia of Mythology*, with an Introduction by Robert Graves (New York, 1959), p. 17.

25. It may be pertinent to note that Demeter and Kore were twin objects of worship at the Eleusinian mysteries, an esoteric cult stressing the fate of the individual soul, in particular personal immortality. See Lewis Spence, *An Encyclopedia of Occultism* (New Hyde Park, 1960), pp. 281–82.

26. Letter to A. G. Troinitsky of July 1, 1868, *Vestnik Evropy*, 1908, No. 12, p. 453.

27. According to the original plan, the idea of "awakening" was to be carried through to the very end. A fragment of an unrealized Part VI, where Sofia Belovodov was to be shown "reborn," indicates that Goncharov had meant to justify his allusion to Chatsky (V, 31) and create in Raysky a contemporary counterpart to Griboedov's hero. He considered the latter as a "sincere and passionate doer" and an "exposer of falsehood and of everything that has grown obsolete, that stifles the new life, the 'free life'" (VIII, 13, 30). See "Nabrosok neosushchestvlennogo prodolzheniia romana *Obryv*," *Literaturnyi arkhiv, III* (Moscow, 1951), 85–90, and *Neobyknovennaia istoriia*, in *op. cit.*, p. 98.

28. *Ocherki i povesti*, pp. 289–93.

29. In his comments on Raysky, Goncharov relates him now to others (VIII, 215–16), now to himself, but with the exception of his own "serious aspects" (VIII, 366). Actually, Raysky bears a strong resemblance to Belinsky's description of the romantic dilettante in his review of *A Common Story* (*I. A. Goncharov v russkoi kritike*, pp. 38–39) as well as to Goncharov's own description of Belinsky, especially his weak points (VIII, 165; *Neobyknovennaia istoriia*, in *op. cit.*, p. 24).

Chapter Six

1. *I. A. Goncharov v russkoi kritike*, pp. 30–31.

2. *Goncharov: Zhizn', lichnost', tvorchestvo*, p. 318.

3. Evgen'ev-Maksimov, *op. cit.*, p. 139.

4. Iulii Aikhenval'd, *Siluety russkikh pisatelei*, 2nd ed. (Moscow, 1908), p. 265.

5. For his minute study of facial characteristics Goncharov may have received some hints from J. C. Lavater, whose work he knew according to A. G. Tseitlin (*Stanovlenie realizma v russkoi literature*, pp. 202–3). Incidentally, the collection in which "Oblomov's Dream" appeared contained an elaborate report on the work of the physiognomists. See *Literaturnyi sbornik*, ed. Sovremennik (St. Petersburg, 1849), pp. 145–210.

6. V. G. Korolenko, in *I. A. Goncharov v russkoi kritike,* p. 330.

7. *Neobyknovennaia istoriia,* in *op. cit.,* p. 17.

8. Stilman, *op. cit.,* pp. 49–50.

9. Aikhenval'd, *op. cit.,* p. 278.

10. Stilman, *op. cit.,* p. 50.

11. Evgen'ev-Maksimov, *op. cit.,* pp. 149–50.

12. Aikhenval'd, *op. cit.,* p. 265.

13. *Op. cit.,* XIII, 253.

14. Though Schiller mentions "imitation of reality" and the "presentation of an ideal" as contrasting possibilities of literary creation, he also says there is a "higher concept which subsumes both," one which coincides with the idea of humanity itself. Significantly, one of Goncharov's thematic ideas, the lack of inner harmony of mind and heart in modern man, is central to Schiller's distinction; this harmony, Schiller thinks, can now only exist "ideally," as moral striving toward unity. ("Über naive und sentimentalische Dichtung," in *Gesammelte Werke,* ed. Reinhold Netolitzky (Bielefeld, 1957), V, 512–13.) This thought seems to underlie Goncharov's "ideal" figures.

15. This "longing" may be related to Goncharov's early interest in Winckelmann's esthetic. A. P. Rybasov says that Stolz and Tushin are "drawn like Hellenes, as perfect human beings revealed according to classical models." (See his Introduction to *Literaturno-kriticheskie stat'i i pis'ma,* p. 38.) Goncharov was well aware of his "idealistic" tendencies. In a letter to Lkhovsky from Marienbad when he was writing *Oblomov* he says: "I am sometimes afraid I don't have a single type, that they are all ideals; will this do?" (VIII, 291).

16. Dobrolyubov, in *I. A. Goncharov v russkoi kritike,* pp. 56–57.

17. *Ibid.,* p. 58.

18. *Op. cit.,* p. 320.

19. Leon Edel, *The Modern Psychological Novel* (New York, 1959), p. 123.

20. The influence of *Oblomov* and Oblomovism is largely limited to Russian literature. Among notable writers, Chekhov deals with similar themes, as in the story "Gooseberries" and in *The Cherry Orchard.* For comment on Gorky's interpretation and treatment of Oblomovism, see Georg Lukács, *Studies in European Realism,* pp. 218–20.

Selected Bibliography

For more extensive listings, the reader is referred to *Istoriia russkoi literatury XIX veka. Bibliograficheskii ukazatel'*, ed. K. D. Muratova (Leningrad, 1962), pp. 247–56, and A. D. Alekseev, *Bibliografiia I. A. Goncharova, 1832–1964* (Leningrad, 1968).

PRIMARY SOURCES

Literaturno-kriticheskie stat'i i pis'ma, ed. A. P. Rybasov. Leningrad, 1938.

Neobyknovennaia istoriia, in *Sbornik Rossiiskoi Publichnoi biblioteki*, II, No. 1. Petrograd, 1924. Pp. 7–189.

Oblomov, tr. Natalie Duddington, with an Introd. by Renato Poggioli. Dutton Paperback. New York, 1960. A lively translation, but with serious omissions.

Oblomov, tr. Ann Dunnigan, with a Foreword by Harry T. Moore. Signet Classics. New York, 1960. The most faithful rendering.

Oblomov, tr. and with an Introd. by David Magarshack. Penguin Classics. Baltimore, 1967. A highly readable translation.

Povesti i ocherki, ed. B. M. Engel'gardt. Leningrad, 1937.

The Same Old Story, tr. Ivy Litvinova. Moscow, 1957. Includes brief excerpts from *Better Late Than Never*.

Sobranie sochinenii, with an Introd. by S. M. Petrov. 8 vols. Moscow, 1952–55.

SECONDARY SOURCES

AIKHENVAL'D, IULII. "Goncharov," in *Siluety russkihk pisatelei*, 2nd ed. (Moscow, 1908), pp. 263–78; also in *The Russian Review*, 1916, Nos. 3 & 4, pp. 108–16, 168–75. A severe but sensitive estimate by a gifted impressionistic critic.

ALEKSEEV, A. D. *Letopis' zhizni i tvorchestva I. A. Goncharova*. M.-L., 1960. An invaluable "chronicle" of Goncharov's personal, official, and literary activities.

ANNENSKII, I. F. "Goncharov i ego Oblomov," *Russkaia shkola*, 1892, No. 4, pp. 71–95. Stresses the visual and contemplative quality of Goncharov's

178 IVAN GONCHAROV

artistic temperament; accents the attractive aspects of Oblomov, such as his lazy "consciousness of his dignity."

BEISOV, P. S. *Goncharov i rodnoi krai.* 2nd ed. Kuibyshev, 1960. An informative study of Goncharov's connection with his native Simbirsk and environs, and their impact on his work.

BRODSKAIA, V. B. "Iazyk i stil' romana I. A. Goncharova *Obyknovennaia istoriia,*" *Voprosy slavianskogo iazykoznaniia,* 1953, No. 3, pp. 129–54; 1955, No. 4, pp. 203–30. A detailed examination of Goncharov's language in *A Common Story.*

CHEMENA, O. M. *Sozdanie dvukh romanov: Goncharov i shestdesiatnitsa E. P. Maikova.* Moscow, 1966. Examines the influence of Catherine Maykov upon Goncharov's work.

DESNITSKII, V. A. "Trilogiia Goncharova," in *Izbrannye stat'i po russkoi literature XVIII–XIX vekov.* M.-L., 1958. Pp. 291–332. A learned but overly elaborate attempt to disprove the thesis of the "vulgar sociologist" V. F. Pereverzev (see below).

EVGEN'EV-MAKSIMOV, V. E. *I. A. Goncharov.* Moscow, 1925. An excellent brief critical study.

GRIGOR'EV, APOLLON. "I. S. Turgenev i ego deiatel'nost'," in *Sobranie sochinenii,* No. 10 (Moscow, 1915), pp. 100–109, 134. A stimulating though rather negative estimate of *A Common Story* and *Oblomov* by an important critic.

I. A. Goncharov v russkoi kritike, with an Introd. by M. I. Poliakov. Moscow, 1958. This collection contains mainly review articles by contemporary radical critics.

I. A. Goncharov v vospominaniiakh sovremennikov, with an Introd. by A. D. Alekseev. Leningrad, 1969. Reminiscences of the author by his contemporaries.

KRASNOSHCHEKOVA, E. *"Oblomov" I. A. Goncharova.* Moscow, 1970. A sensitive reading of the novel, with emphasis on the psychological and moral complexity of Goncharov's characters.

LABRIOLLE, FRANÇOIS DE. "Oblomov n'est-il qu'un paresseux?," *Cahiers du monde russe et soviétique,* X (1969), No. 1, pp. 38–51. A good psychological study of the personality of Oblomov.

LAVRIN, J. *Goncharov.* New Haven, 1954. A brief, judicious assessment of Goncharov's achievement.

LIATSKII, E. A. *Goncharov: Zhizn', lichnost', tvorchestvo.* 3rd ed. Stockholm, 1920. "Critical-biographical sketches" aimed chiefly at proving the "subjective" inspiration of Goncharov's fiction. Valid insights despite a questionable methodology which blurs the distinction between the man and the artist.

———. *Roman i zhizn'.* Prague, 1925. Subtitled the "development of I. A. Goncharov's creative personality," this book, which covers the years

1812–57, is the first volume of a projected biography that was never completed.

MAYS, MILTON A. "Oblomov as Anti-Faust," *Western Humanities Review*, XXI (1967), 141–52. Sees Oblomov as a new archetype related to Freud's ego instinct as opposed to Faust, viewed as an embodiment of the sexual instinct.

MAZON, ANDRÉ. *Un maître du roman russe: Ivan Gontcharov*. Paris, 1914. A great work of scholarship, this book, organized on the "life and works" principle, is still an invaluable aid to the student of Goncharov. Includes a great many documents pertaining to Goncharov's work as a censor.

MEREZHKOVSKII, D. S. "Goncharov," in *Polnoe sobranie sochinenii*, XIII: *Vechnye sputniki* (St. Petersburg-Moscow, 1911), pp. 237–60. First published as an article in 1890, this critique presents Goncharov as a calm epic portrayer highly sensitive to the "poetry of the past." Occasionally sentimental, idealizing.

MOSER, CHARLES. *Anti-nihilism in the Russian Novel of the 1860's*. The Hague, 1964. Discusses antinihilistic elements in *The Precipice*.

OVSIANIKO-KULIKOVSKII, D. N. *Istoriia russkoi intelligentsii*, Pt. 1. 6th ed., in *Sobranie sochinenii* (Moscow, 1923–24), VII, 194–230. Interprets Oblomovism as a malady of the Russian national psyche.

PEREVERZEV, V. F. "Sotsial'nyi genezis oblomovshchiny," *Pechat' i revoliutsia*, 1925, No. 2, pp. 61–78. One of several articles in which the critic argues that Goncharov's heroes express the patriarchal-bourgeois crisis at the coming of capitalism; the gentry elements in Goncharov's novels are seen as a "masquerade" for bourgeois themes.

PIKSANOV, N. K. *Roman Goncharova "Obryv" v svete sotsial'noi istorii*. Leningrad, 1968. A healthy antidote to Soviet critical eulogies of Goncharov's last novel.

POLITYKO, D. A. *Roman I. A. Goncharova "Obryv."* Minsk, 1962. A detailed study of *The Precipice*, including its "creative history" and its relation to the antinihilist novel.

PRITCHETT, V. S. "The Great Absentee," in *The Living Novel* (London, 1946), pp. 233–40. A witty and enthusiastic essay on *Oblomov*, stressing the book's subjective inspiration and the profound meaning of the title figure, particularly his appeal to our "secret desire."

PRUTSKOV, N. I. *Masterstvo Goncharova-romanista*. Moscow, 1962. Excellent structural analysis, especially of *Oblomov;* the treatment of *The Precipice* is much less satisfactory. The critic brilliantly contrasts Goncharov's style with that of several of his contemporaries.

RAPP, HELEN. "The Art of Ivan Goncharov," *The Slavonic and East European Review*, XXXVI (June, 1958), 370–95. Perceptive discussion of the cardinal features of Goncharov's technique.

REHM, WALTHER. "Gontscharow und die Langeweile," in *Experimentum Medietatis* (Munich, 1947), pp. 96–183. An interesting philosophical study of Goncharov's treatment of boredom, especially in *The Precipice*. But the estimate of the novel is uncritical, particularly in regard to the handling of the double narrative perspective.

RYBASOV, A. P. *Goncharov.* Moscow, 1957. A well-written popular study, though somewhat spoiled by excessive national pathos.

————. *I. A. Goncharov.* Moscow, 1962. A handy abbreviated version of the preceding book.

SABUROV, A. A. *Voina i mir L. N. Tolstogo: Problematika i poetika.* Moscow, 1959. Contains an excellent characterization of Goncharov's dialogue as contrasted with that of Turgenev and Tolstoy.

STILMAN, LEON. "Oblomovka Revisited," *American Slavic and East European Review*, VII (1948), 45–77. Taking his point of departure in Liatskii's theory of Goncharov's subjective inspiration, the author works out a psychoanalytically-tinged interpretation of Goncharov's creative personality.

TSEITLIN, A. G. *I. A. Goncharov.* Moscow, 1950. An exhaustive critical monograph; good, but occasionally plodding. Indispensable to any serious student of Goncharov.

ZAKHARKIN, A. F. *Roman I. A. Goncharova "Oblomov."* Moscow, 1963. A poorly organized study; but it contains a convenient brief survey of *Oblomov* criticism and illustrates Goncharov's careful revision of his manuscript.

Index

182

IVAN GONCHAROV